READY, WILLING,
AND ABLE

READY, WILLING, AND ABLE

A Developmental Approach to College Access and Success

MANDY SAVITZ-ROMER

SUZANNE M. BOUFFARD

Harvard Education Press

Cambridge, Massachusetts

Library of Congress Control Number 2011941945

Paperback ISBN: 978-1-61250-132-1
Library Edition ISBN: 978-1-61250-133-8

Published by Harvard Education Press,
an imprint of the Harvard Education Publishing Group

Harvard Education Press
8 Story Street
Cambridge, MA 02138

Cover Design: Sarah Henderson

The typefaces used in this book are Legacy Serif ITC and Knockout.

CONTENTS

INTRODUCTION

Redefining College Readiness

The story of American higher education is a story about opportunity. But in more than twenty-five years of combined experience working with young people, we have seen our share of missed opportunities. Despite our and our colleagues' good intentions and hard work, and despite many successes, we have seen too many young people who had the potential to attend college fall through the cracks. Ronaldo was one of these students.

❖   ❖   ❖

As a ninth-grader, Ronaldo was charismatic, intelligent, and, to his teacher, Ms. Contreras, he often seemed wise beyond his fifteen years. Ronaldo spent most of his time with kids he described as his "crew" rather than kids in her class. Ms. Contreras knew that some of these youth did not take school seriously, and some were even known gang members. Unlike them, Ronaldo came to class every day and participated thoughtfully. But he sometimes had a cavalier attitude and failed to turn in homework that he could have completed easily. Drawn to his charismatic personality and convinced of his potential, Ms. Contreras wanted to help Ronaldo get on an academic path, so she referred him to a college preparation program at a local college, hoping that this would help him establish a college-going identity.

To Ms. Contreras's delight, Ronaldo participated in the spring semester of the program and began to talk about the possibility of going to college. At the end of the term, he received all Bs on his report card (a marked improvement from the fall). After much encouragement, he also signed up for the summer component, a six-week campus live-in program, despite his concern that he "didn't belong there."

When school began the following fall, Ms. Contreras was disappointed to learn that Ronaldo had never completed the program. A few weeks into the session, the program director had discovered graffiti on a classroom wall and accused Ronaldo of tagging. Ronaldo was adamant that he had had nothing to do with the incident, and he was insulted by the director's accusation, which he felt was based on the way he dressed and spoke. After initially trying to advocate for himself in a positive way, Ronaldo eventually cursed at the program director and stormed out. Although he had the option to apologize or clean up the graffiti, Ronaldo felt that this would have falsely affirmed that he had done something wrong, and he left the program instead.

When Ms. Contreras pulled the story out of Ronaldo (after many inquiries and much prodding), he summed up his experience by saying that people in the program "didn't see me," by which he meant that they didn't see him as he saw himself—as a responsible person headed for a bright future. Looking back, Ms. Contreras realized that Ronaldo had often said similar things to her about other teachers and staff in the school.

During the years following this experience, Ronaldo became more and more immersed in the gang culture to which his friends belonged and less connected to school. It seemed that the way others saw him, or failed to see him, began to affect how he saw himself. Eventually, Ronaldo transferred to an alternative high school, where he struggled for several years until finally graduating with no future plans. Ms. Contreras often worried that she had been wrong in referring him to the college preparation program in ninth grade and wondered what she could have done differently.

Like Ms. Contreras, many caring, dedicated practitioners are left scratching their heads. In classrooms, college access and youth development programs, and college admissions offices all around the country, professionals wonder, "What went wrong?" and "How did I lose that young person?" Many are particularly concerned about how to boost the enrollment of young people who are traditionally underrepresented in and face significant barriers to higher education.

At the same time, many of us also have stories of youth who surprised us and reminded us just how possible—and valuable—it is for youth at risk of low educational attainment to make it to and succeed in college. Another ninth-grader, named Lashai, illustrates this kind of story.

Ninth-grade counselor Mr. White was at a loss. One of his assigned students, Lashai, was constantly resisting his efforts to talk about her academics, her afterschool activities, or her future goals. Lashai was smart and strong willed but totally uninterested in

talking about her future. She came to school every day and had many friends, but she appeared to have no interest in academics and mostly skated by with Ds. Mr. White persisted in trying to engage her, but he felt as though nothing he did worked. Moreover, he knew that there were other students in his caseload of 450 who actually wanted his time. Eventually, Mr. White scaled back his efforts and settled on an amicable but unproductive relationship with Lashai.

At the end of her junior year, Lashai unexpectedly bounced into Mr. White's office to report that she wanted to go to college. That day, Mr. White and Lashai began a detailed conversation about the necessary preparation for college that continued into her senior year. As a senior, Lashai's report cards demonstrated what Mr. White and his colleagues had known all along: with clear goals, Lashai could achieve academically. With A's (and the occasional B) on her report card, and an articulate sense of her newfound purpose, Lashai was accepted to a local college to study social work.

Mr. White was never able to pinpoint when and why everything had changed for Lashai. "How can I help other students experience the same transformation when I'm not sure what helped her?" he wondered.

Mr. White was aware that something beyond his diligent efforts was at work with Lashai. But he was at a loss to explain it or to leverage it so that he could help other young people like Lashai in the future. Here was another missed opportunity—not for Lashai, but for Mr. White's other students.

Stories like Ronaldo's and Lashai's are common. And the questions facing the adults in their lives—about why youth do or do not succeed even when significant resources are available—constitute some of the most important and challenging issues in promoting college access and success. As most educators and youth professionals know, there are many talented young people who arrive in programs, classrooms, and offices with clear and focused goals that make it seem like they are living and breathing college. But it is those who do not already have these inclinations and habits—but who are clearly bright and talented—who adults most need to reach. Some of those youth muddle along with little focus and then, like Lashai, find their drive and marshal internal resources that had been building over time. But others, like Ronaldo, get lost. Some dream early and often of going to college, but they behave in ways that, at best, don't support these goals and, at worst, belie their true goals, leaving homework undone, missing deadlines, and opting out of available programs. Even more troubling, many youth prematurely decide that college is not for them, sometimes as early as middle school, even before having the chance to explore their options. These examples—of which there are many more—leave teachers, counselors, youth workers, parents, and others wondering, "What happened?"

THE ESSENTIAL BUT OFTEN INVISIBLE ROLE OF ADOLESCENT DEVELOPMENT

While there are many reasons that promising youth don't enroll and succeed in higher education, we believe that one of the primary reasons has been left unexplored. Simply put, one of the answers to the "what happened?" question is this: adolescent development happened. Anyone who works with middle school and high school youth knows that they experience significant growth. While physical changes are the easiest to see in this age group, most adults are aware that social and emotional changes are also occurring rapidly, as evidenced by an increase in the importance of peers and an increasing desire for independence. It is quite logical that such developmental changes matter a great deal in adolescents' college-going choices and behaviors. Yet to date, college preparation and planning efforts have paid little attention to the role of social, emotional, and cognitive development, especially to the questions of *how* these developmental changes matter and how they should impact practitioners' work with youth.

For example, many adults know that adolescents are constantly experimenting and grappling with their identities. But many college access efforts and practitioners fail to think about whether and how young people develop college-going identities, or assume that they already have them. Take, for instance, the growing trend to have schools adopt a "College Day" in which faculty and staff wear college sweatshirts and hang college pennants with the goal of inspiring students to think about and aim for college. For a young person who doesn't hold college-goer as part of his identity or who thinks "I'm not 'college material,'" seeing others with college sweatshirts probably does very little to promote aspirations. In contrast, if the College Day is coupled with other developmentally appropriate strategies designed to help youth envision college-going futures, the sweatshirts and pennants could provide a good reminder and a validation that others around them have similar goals.

Similarly, practitioners who work with young people often have a cursory awareness of the processes that support college-going goals and motivations, assuming that motivation is a simple yes or no quality. A lack of understanding about motivational processes, especially about how different kinds of goals can help or hurt in the long run, can actually undermine the very outcomes that practitioners are trying to promote. One of us remembers her early days of attempting to motivate students for college simply by telling them about the careers that they could hold with a bachelor's degree or the increasing amount of money they could make across their lifetimes. While those motivators may have helped some students, they didn't reach everyone. In fact, research suggests that focusing solely on extrinsic reasons like these might have even made the youth who responded to them less likely to succeed and graduate once they were in college than if they had been motivated by more personal reasons.

Even skill development, the backbone of many college access efforts, could benefit from a more intentional focus on adolescent development. Practitioners who talk about skill development are usually focused on reading, writing, critical thinking, and other academic skills. Indeed, navigating a successful college-going path requires that youth develop these skills, and this is why the vast majority of college access programs include a tutoring component. However, self-regulation skills, such as focusing, planning, organizing, and reflecting, are also crucial skills that lay the foundation for these academic skills and for many parts of the college-going process.

Despite their importance, these developmental skills and processes have received little attention among practitioners who prepare young people for college. This is a missed opportunity at best, and one that is easier to change than many people may think.

A NEW APPROACH

In this book, we call for a new approach to college access and success, one that emphasizes key developmental tasks and processes of adolescence and that integrates them into existing practices in meaningful ways. We believe that practitioners must be deliberate in their efforts to stimulate and leverage social, emotional, and cognitive aspects of adolescent development in order to engage more young people in college planning and also to prepare them for success once in college. This focus should complement and build a foundation for the academic, informational, aspirational, and financial supports that make up current college access practices. This book makes explicit some of the connections that have been missing between adolescent development and college access, drawing on decades of research and theory. Based on our experience in both practice and research, it also describes how these connections give rise to concrete strategies for engaging young people—especially low-income students and first-generation college-bound students—in developing and realizing postsecondary aspirations and opportunities.

Our interest in and commitment to the topics explored in this book have grown from of our years of experience as practitioners, researchers, trainers, professors, and students ourselves. We both share an interest in youth development and educational equity, with a special focus on practitioner professional development and training. However, each of us comes to this work from a different place. Mandy is a former school counselor, college access professional, administrator, and current faculty member at the Harvard Graduate School of Education. She has a long-standing interest in college readiness and how schools can structure effective college access and readiness counseling and support. Suzanne brings to this book a background in developmental psychology, experience working with youth in arts and afterschool programs, and a focus on providing research-informed professional development to practitioners. Her work is dedicated to bridging the worlds of research, practice, and policy by making theory and research accessible to those who most need it and can benefit from it. For both of us, this book affords us an opportunity to speak to questions and concerns that we hear from graduate students, practitioners, and policy makers, and to help them enhance their already dedicated efforts. It is also a chance to share the kinds of struggles and opportunities we have experienced and witnessed, which we do, in part, by presenting case examples inspired by (and sometimes aggregated across) real youth and practitioners. Our hope is that these stories, along with a clearer understanding of developmental theory and research, will better equip practitioners to support youth like Lashai and Ronaldo by helping practitioners meet youth where they are, whether that is at the beginning or end of—or not yet even in sight of—a college-going path.

This developmental perspective on college access is needed more today than ever before. Attaining a college degree today is a challenging and complex process that starts long before youth apply to college and continues after they enter. This is reflected in the fact that youth practitioners, higher education administrations, and policy makers define college access and success as a broad set of tasks that span settings and time. These include aspiration, preparation, application, matriculation, and, finally, graduation. Across these stages, young people need multiple supports and resources in order to develop the social, emotional, and cognitive skills that they need to successfully navigate the process.

But many young people lack the supports they need to develop these skills. As counselors and others who work with youth know, college access programs and practices have focused almost exclusively on providing information, academic preparation, and financial support. While these efforts are clearly important, they are not enough to ensure the success of the young people who are currently least likely to access and graduate from college. The challenges for these youth are magnified by the fact that many college access initiatives rely on youth having already developed the personal resources, such as motivation and a college-going identity, that will enable them to benefit from other programmatic resources. What is missing from current efforts is attention to helping youth develop these personal resources and internal capacities. Without this, the most vulnerable young people don't just miss the boat; they aren't even on the dock.

We believe that this expanded approach is particularly important for working with youth who are traditionally underrepresented in higher education and for closing the gaps in educational equity that we describe in chapter 1. Here we focus largely on first-generation college-bound students whose parents and other family members have not gone to college and who are particularly at risk of missing out on higher education. In our experience, first-generation college-bound students need as much support as possible to help them overcome the many challenges they face, which often include the stresses associated with low family income and under-resourced communities, limited access to high-quality educational resources, and structural and social barriers like racism and classism. At the same time, the processes and strategies described in this book are applicable to a wide range of young people and practitioners. For example, we delve into issues such as the role of racial and ethnic identity that may be particularly common among first-generation college-bound students but that are central for many youth.

The absence of connections between adolescent development and college access initiatives that we see today can be traced, in part, to training and in-service programs for practitioners. A diverse group of practitioners is engaged in the processes of preparing young people for college, including counselors, teachers, afterschool leaders, youth workers, and others. Many of these practitioners come from pathways that lack sufficient training in adolescent development. In other cases, even when development is a primary focus, there is a lack of connection to college planning and preparation. For example, a cadre of community-based practitioners who may be trained in principles of youth development rarely receive training related to promoting college-going behaviors and choices. Nonprofit agencies often employ college students or recent graduates who come from a range of academic backgrounds, often completely outside of the education and social service realms. As a result, they must rely entirely on in-service professional development, which tends to emphasize the instrumental processes associated with college-going. These gaps in training present challenges, but, as we describe, there are opportunities before and during direct service work to think and act in more developmentally aware ways.

DEFINING COLLEGE ACCESS AND SUCCESS

We explore the processes and strategies that can support what we describe as *college-going behaviors* or *college access and success*. We have chosen these terms based on three primary factors. First, our focus includes college success (completion of a degree) as well as access (enrollment and matriculation). Second, in a nation with a highly diverse system of higher education, we use the term *college* to refer to a variety of postsecondary educational options. Third, while our focus in this book is on higher education, the developmental processes and strategies we describe enable young people to pursue multiple viable postsecondary pathways, including not just college but postsecondary careers that do not require a degree. We describe each of these principles in more detail.

Access to a College Degree

If we have learned anything from our diverse experiences in practice and policy, it is that college access is not genuine if it does not lead to a degree. In other words, simply getting more youth accepted to college is insufficient, especially for first-generation college students and other students from groups traditionally underrepresented in higher education, all of whom are particularly at risk of leaving college prior to attaining a degree. Providing young people supports that do not take into consideration future obstacles is akin to a GPS device directing a driver onto a highway only to leave the driver to figure out the rest of the journey on his own.

The principles of adolescent development that we explore are applicable to all stages of college-going, and we describe their potential to simultaneously build young people's capacity to enroll and succeed in higher education. Some of these processes are particularly applicable to either access or success. For example, in chapter 3 we describe how envisioning oneself as a college student helps young people begin college planning. On the other end of the spectrum, in chapter 5, we explain how attending college for intrinsic reasons can make students more likely to persist in the face of obstacles, such as introductory courses that are challenging and sometimes seem dry or boring.

Even though some readers may work at only one stage in the college pipeline (and some may work with youth before or after adolescence), understanding how development affects all phases of college-going is important. As we describe in chapter 2, development is a continuous process, and practitioners who work at all points in the college pipeline therefore need to have an understanding of how their work is connected to other points along the pipeline. If high school practitioners don't understand how some reasons for attending college can cause problems in the long run, their hard work may not pay off. If college administrators don't understand how identity lays a foundation for access, they may target their recruitment efforts ineffectively or miss opportunities to help students who struggle in their first year of college.

A Broad Definition of College

In the film *National Lampoon's Animal House*, John "Bluto" Blutarsky, played by John Belushi, wears a sweatshirt that

looks like a typical college pride sweatshirt, except that it pro-
claims only COLLEGE, with nothing to specify which college.
For Bluto, and for many people, college represents one kind of
place and one kind of experience. However, the reality is quite
the opposite. According to U.S. Census data, the United States
is home to more than four thousand degree-granting colleges
and universities, which vary by defining features, including:
public and private; two- and four-year; residential and com-
muter; not-for-profit and for-profit; liberal arts and specialized
institutions; and minority-serving institutions. Our use of the
term *college* is explicitly intended to describe postsecondary education in its many forms.

We also use *college* to focus on higher education and not explicitly on careers. Many programs, practices, and policies use
"college and career" readiness to reflect postsecondary destina-
tions. Merging these two concepts has some advantages, especially in light of the fact that college-going can be viewed as a
step in one's broader career development. Indeed, the processes
we describe in this book influence career choices, interests, and
actions as well as college-going. However, our emphasis is on
college, because much has been written in the field of career development that ties developmental processes to career and vocational choices, whereas college-going has not benefited from the
same kinds of clear connections to developmental literature.

College for All or College for Some?

An important debate taking place nationally and in many states
is whether practitioners should focus on preparing all young
people for college or also include attention to career pathways
that do not require a college degree. This debate is driven in
part by questions about whether "college for all" philosophies

are both warranted and realistic. An unintended consequence of extensive public and policy interest in postsecondary success has been, until recently, a unilateral focus on college as the only viable pathway. More recently, however, some critics have begun to argue that charter schools and other secondary schools focusing on college preparation (and opting to use college enrollment as a measure of success) are falling prey to the education reform du jour. And others have begun to openly question whether this focus fails to value the teaching of knowledge and skills necessary for vocational pathways. In their report, *Pathways to Prosperity*, our colleagues at the Harvard Graduate School of Education, Robert Schwartz, Ronald Ferguson, and William Symonds, challenge the notion of college for all, advocating instead for models of education that offer and support multiple postsecondary pathways from adolescence through adulthood. They argue that current efforts have narrowly focused on one pathway to success, which works for some youth but fails to respond to the diversity of youth and the needs of a twenty-first-century economy, and that developing more individualized pathways requires a holistic approach to supporting youth development.[1]

Indeed, young people have different strengths and interests, and they need and deserve to be supported and well-prepared to follow the paths for which they are best suited. However, one cannot argue with the fact that the majority of today's jobs require advanced skills and credentials, typically acquired through higher education, and that all young people therefore deserve the opportunity to explore college as an option—even if it is one that they choose not to pursue.

The intention behind this book is not to take sides with either a college-for-all or a multiple-pathways approach. There is mounting evidence that there is less distinction today than there used to be between the skills that support college and career readiness. And the developmental processes described in this book are no exception. The processes and strategies we describe can and should be leveraged to promote multiple forms of postsecondary success. However, this book does focus intentionally on college, because it is our firm conviction that all youth should have the chance to *consider* college as an option, and we believe that a lack of attention to the developmental processes described in this book, such as identity and self regulation, is one of the reasons that many young people never get that chance.

USING THIS BOOK

Our aim in writing this book was to support practitioners to better prepare all young people, especially those who may not already see themselves as "college material" or possess college-going goals, who seem off-track in their future planning, or who are vulnerable to postsecondary attrition. Because the efforts of adults in many roles and many settings are necessary and valuable, this book is written for professionals who support college access and success at multiple levels, including those who work directly with youth in schools and community settings, program directors, faculty members who prepare practitioners in graduate programs and professional development agencies, and those who make and implement policy. In the chapters that follow, we describe strategies that can be used by counselors, teachers, youth workers, and others, and we share case examples that involve professionals from many of these diverse roles.

Having worked in some of these roles ourselves, we recognize that the daily responsibilities of practitioners are demanding and full. Our aim is not to suggest an "add-on" approach to practitioners' current work, but rather to suggest in some places a "different than" or "as part of" approach. A developmental approach can be applied at all times, from shaping specific activities and programming to influencing everyday decisions and ways of interacting with youth. For example, in chapter 5, we describe how praising students for their academic successes based on effort rather than innate ability ("Great job! You must have worked really hard!" versus "Great job! See how smart you are?") can make young people more likely to persist when they encounter challenges. In chapter 6, we suggest ways that practitioners can help young people take ownership of the college-going process by giving them responsibility for key preparation tasks, even when it is easier for the adults to complete those tasks themselves (such as mailing applications rather than repeatedly reminding young people to do it). Practitioners engaged at many points in the college-going pipeline will find ways to enhance their practice, whether their efforts are focused on raising young people's postsecondary aspirations, disseminating college knowledge, or providing academic preparation.

Our goal is not to make readers experts in theory or to create a comprehensive encyclopedia of research. Rather, we aim to help practitioners from a variety of backgrounds approach their work in a way that recognizes the centrality of adolescent development and the potential power of applying it to practice. We focus on a few key processes that are vital to college-going and yet underemphasized: identity development, self-concept and aspirations, motivation and goal-setting, self-regulatory skills, and relationship development. Our discussion of all of these processes is based on a foundation of key principles from developmental science. As we describe in chapter 2, these principles include the fact that development in general and college-going in particular develop within environmental contexts and social relationships, over time, and in distinct but interconnected stages. Research has shown us that, while all stages matter, adolescence is a stage that is particularly relevant for college access and success and, as we emphasize, that adolescents can and should take ownership of the college-going process, becoming active agents in constructing their own futures.

This book is organized in a way that is designed both to illuminate specific developmental processes and to show how they are interrelated and build on one another, providing strategies and tips throughout. The first chapter describes the need for a developmental perspective and includes a summary of the challenges facing practitioners in promoting college access today, the barriers to higher education faced by first-generation and other underserved students, and the reasons that innovative and developmentally aware strategies are needed to engage those youth still falling through the cracks in the K–16 pipeline. Chapter 2 defines what we mean by a developmental approach, describes the key developmental principles on which the book is founded, and shares a brief overview of the youth development research and literature that is applied throughout the book.

Chapters 3 through 7 are organized around core developmental processes and principles that are primary to postsecondary aspiration formation, planning, and attainment. The chapters examine each of these principles in turn and offer explicit discussion of how they are connected with specific postsecondary planning and preparation tasks. Chapter 3 draws on psychological theories that describe the processes of identity development and explains how these processes influence whether or not a young person comes to see himself as a college-goer. Chapter 4 focuses on how adolescents' self-concepts and beliefs about their abilities shape college preparation, planning, and other college-going behaviors. Chapter 5 explores why certain kinds of goals are more beneficial than others for long-term educational success and explains how the views of self described in chapters 3 and 4 influence not just whether young people pursue college but why. Chapter 6 highlights the important but underacknowledged role of self-regulation in college access and success through such behaviors as staying on task in school, utilizing the organizational and planning skills necessary for applying to college, delaying gratification, and staying the course in the face of difficulties and hardships. Chapter 7 focuses on the role of relationships, describing how positive relationships with peers and family members can support the processes described in the previous chapters. In the conclusion, we draw on the ideas and processes presented to offer a set of principles that we believe should be incorporated into programs, practices, and approaches that support college access in more holistic and effective ways.

Adolescent development is a wide-ranging topic, the full scope of which is well beyond this book. It is also important to note that development is not a linear process. All of the developmental processes we describe are cyclical and interactive. Across the chapters, we present specific aspects of development in a linear fashion for ease of reading, but practitioners do not need to be address them in the order in which we present them here. We expect that readers will find that some youth need more support in one area than another (e.g., goal-setting or self-regulation) and that some will benefit from establishing a strong foundation in one area (e.g., identity or relationships) before focusing on other areas.

GETTING STARTED

This book calls for change—change in the way adults think about engaging young people in planning for a positive future. It suggests a reinvention of the college access and success system in a way that considers a developmental dimension that has rarely been incorporated in this work due to lack of training and resources. Such change is vital if we are to raise and realize the aspirations and postsecondary accomplishments that our society has set for young people. This is especially critical for young people who lack social networks that otherwise build college-going aspirations, beliefs, and behaviors, including, but not limited to, first-generation college-bound students. The principles and strategies we describe here could create a new foundation for college access efforts, so that youth like Ronaldo and Lashai will have solid supports to stand on and will not fall through the cracks. With these young people and so many others like them in mind, we invite you to start building.

PART I

Changing the Conversation

1

MORE YOUTH, MORE READY

*A Developmental Understanding of Gaps
in Educational Equity*

In 1995, I (Mandy) began my career as a ninth-grade school counselor at an urban high school in Boston. Primarily charged with providing early college awareness, I marveled at the chance to reach students early and ensure that they had access to an array of postsecondary information and planning opportunities. Without the pressure of applications and deadlines that mark the senior year or the challenges of working with young people at the end of the secondary school experience, the opportunities seemed endless—these were young people whose futures had yet to be invented. During an early fall workshop that I led in the school's newly created College and Career Center, I asked a group of thirty-one freshmen, "How many of you see yourselves going to college?" Looking at the students with hands in the air, I felt a mix of emotions. On one hand, I was delighted to see twenty-three ninth-graders, most of whom would be first in their families to go to college, show interest in postsecondary education. On the other hand, I couldn't understand why eight of these ninth-graders had already decided not to go to college at such a young age. It seemed that for some reason they had already come to believe that college was either not necessary or not possible. Over time, my delight in many of the other twenty-three hands diminished as well. Noticing that some of those were either failing classes or rarely attending school, I started questioning the authenticity of their college aspirations. Later, when I was assigned to tenth-, eleventh-, and twelfth-graders, I encountered similar students who had ruled out going to college or who showed misalignment between their aspirations and their behaviors.

At the time, neither I nor my colleagues could figure out what was missing. As a school, the right supports seemed to be in place. We had a principal committed to college and career awareness, evidenced by both a dedicated counselor focused on early college awareness and the fact that the school was home to the city's first college and career center. In addition, a strong school-university partnership and links to a wide range of college preparatory and enrichment opportunities were well established. Many of the teachers participated in college planning activities. Yet even with all of this in place, many of our thirteen hundred students would eventually fail to pursue higher education.

Fifteen years later, things look different than they did that day in the College and Career Center. Most notably, the range of people and organizations committed to supporting college planning and preparation has expanded. Today, the organizations and institutions explicitly targeting college access and success include K–12 schools, innovative precollege programs, a range of youth development organizations, campus-based programs, and a host of educational reform initiatives. This wide community of caring and hard-working adults also has the benefit of more knowledge about the challenges to and effective strategies for working with first-generation college-bound youth.

Yet the number of young people entering college from high schools like the one where I worked is still low, and educational statistics confirm what many of us see every day: low-income, ethnic minority, and first-generation college-bound youth are significantly less likely than their peers to apply to, matriculate into, and graduate from institutions of higher education. According to the National Center for Education Statistics, while undergraduate enrollment increased by approximately 24 percent between 2000 and 2009, persistent gaps can still be seen across racial, ethnic, and income groups. Data from 2008 show that 90 percent of Asian students and 71 percent of white students enrolled in college immediately after high school, as compared to 63 percent of black and 62 percent of Hispanic students. Gaps across income levels are even more stark: in 2009, 84 percent of youth from high-income families enrolled immediately after high school, compared with 55 percent of those from low-income families, a twenty-nine percentage point difference. (Even high school graduates from middle-income families lagged behind at 67 percent.)[1] And the gaps widen as young people make their way through the educational pipeline. For example, according to the Education Trust, approximately six out of ten enrolled white students earn bachelor's degrees, as compared with only about four out of ten enrolled minority students.[2]

These gaps persist due to many factors. Policy reports usually cite poor schooling, inadequate college counseling, parents and caretakers who are inexperienced with college-going, mounting tuition costs, and young people's limited aspirations and lack of knowledge about the college-going process. Research from the fields of education, psychology, economics, sociology, and public policy has shown that young people facing these barriers need multiple supports: strong academic preparation, financial literacy and aid, high educational expectations, and college readiness counseling and support. This research has given rise to many wonderful college access programs and organizations, new school-based practices, and educational policies that are making a big difference in the lives and futures of youth all around the country. But the statistics make it clear that more is needed.

We believe that attention to adolescent development is one of the big things that is missing. After gaining experience in the fields of higher education, youth development, and prevention science, I (Mandy) realized that my and my colleagues' practices failed to take into account identity, motivation, peer relationships, and other developmental processes that are so central for adolescents. Practitioners are not the only ones responsible for these missed connections—or for redressing them. As a researcher, I (Suzanne) have seen, and even published, some valuable research on youth development that has sat on bookshelves, never making it into the hands of the practitioners who could use it most. This happens partially because the researchers who conduct it don't reach out to practitioners and because they often don't present it in ways that are applicable to everyday practice. My reading of the research, in combination with experiences working with young people in afterschool and arts programs, has convinced me that by forging these connections between developmental research and practice, young people will have more of the supports they need to enroll in and succeed in college. I'm also convinced that applying a developmental perspective to college access doesn't necessarily require working more, but rather working differently.

Practitioners, policy and practice leaders, and researchers all need training and time to make connections between developmental research and practice. They also need opportunities to make those connections real. The good news is that today there is great public interest in and attention to the topic of college access and success, which provides a window of opportunity for building and using a more coherent developmental approach. But realizing this potential requires understanding several limitations to current efforts and seeing how a developmental approach can help. Below we describe the state of the field of college access and success, with a particular focus on challenges facing practitioners and where using a developmental framework can strengthen current efforts and promote the educational equity that young people deserve.

ADDRESSING THE CHALLENGES

In our experience working with and for youth—in school counseling, youth programs, research and policy, and preservice education—we have never seen more interest in helping low-income, first-generation college-bound students gain access to a college degree. When one of us recently gave a talk to a select group of graduate students representing thirteen different master's degree programs, all of the students in attendance expressed a unique interest in the topic of college access, despite representing different educational areas, points of entry, and positions within the field of education. This, we believe, is due in large part to the tremendous interest today in preparing *all* young people for postsecondary opportunities, and an agreement that we *all* share responsibility for this goal. This surge of interest has been driven largely by national calls for improved degree attainment, increased awareness of inequities across the preK–16 pipeline, a shift in responsibility for college success, and the increasing need for postsecondary credentials for economic security and global competitiveness.

But despite the interest and resources, we see three primary challenges hindering progress. First, current efforts have a relatively narrow focus that does not meet all of youths' needs. Second, much of the current programming is designed to serve young people who already have the motivation and initiative to attend college. There is little attention paid to reaching those who could succeed in college but aren't knocking on practitioners' office doors or applying for programs because they don't envision themselves as college-goers. And third, the diversity of professionals and settings involved in this work, while encouraging, raises questions about whether practitioners have the kinds of training and competencies required to support youth effectively. As we describe below, a developmental perspective on college access and success can help practitioners and policy makers address all of these challenges.

A Limited Focus in College Preparation Efforts

Schools and organizations committed to promoting college access and success typically tailor their efforts to address the gaps in academics, financial knowledge, and college information that otherwise limit young people's future goals and planning. Most commonly, practices and programs target academic preparation, aspiration formation, college knowledge and planning, and financial support.

The academic arena has probably garnered the most attention. Indeed, evidence suggests that academic preparation is the most accurate predictor of whether or not a young person will enroll and succeed in college. Academic readiness for college has been defined in many ways and promoted through multiple strategies, from encouraging students to take a college-preparatory curriculum, to aligning standards and curricula in a K–16 approach, to promoting study habits that enable success in college and work. For example, in his book *College Knowledge*, David Conley stresses the importance of cultivating the knowledge, skills, and cognitive strategies necessary for college enrollment and success.[3]

Many college access programs and practices also target youths' educational aspirations (hopes and dreams) and expectations (beliefs about their futures). One of the reasons aspirations and expectations play such a key role is because research suggests that too many youth rule out college as an option simply because they cannot see themselves as "college material." It is common for precollege programs to stress high college-going expectations and to use mentors and inspirational messaging to shape aspirations, expectations, and, ideally, college-going identities. This emphasis is also evident among public media campaigns that utilize television, social media, and other technology to communicate the importance of higher education.

In addition to aspirations, practitioners who work with young people to support postsecondary planning often focus heavily on college knowledge and awareness. This theme is the cornerstone of many college access programs, partially in response to concerns that misinformation might lead to lowered expectations and aspirations and decrease the likelihood of college success. Essential college knowledge includes information about postsecondary opportunities, educational requirements, experiences, and costs. One of the reasons that this area is a focus for programs serving first-generation college students is that these students' parents do not already have postsecondary experiences and knowledge and their children therefore need to obtain this college knowledge from other sources. One of the most promising and well-documented models of providing postsecondary information and awareness is the establishment of a college-going culture. According to Patricia McDonough, who first operationalized this term, when a school establishes a college-going culture, it sends frequent messages and information about college-going through the efforts of many staff and at many times, so that college-going information is in the drinking water, so to speak.

A growing number of school programs and college preparation organizations are turning their attention to financial literacy and support. Many professionals have pointed out the importance of providing financial literacy to youth early in their aspiration formation and decision making so that they do not close off the possibility of college prematurely and also so that they have the skills for making good economic decisions. Programmatic emphasis on financial aid support and assistance is driven by research showing that many youth make postsecondary decisions in the absence of accurate financial information. These decisions include whether one goes to college, if one completes federal financial aid forms, and where one attends college.

While these kinds of activities are clearly valuable, we believe that there is a glaring omission in current efforts, a lack of attention to the personal resources and capacities that *actively* engage young people in the process of getting to and through college. This point was conveyed recently by an American Youth Policy Forum report, which argued that:

> The traditional view of college-readiness, which has for many students meant a focus on improved academic performance, may fail to fully capture the developmental processes required for youth to enter, succeed in, and graduate from postsecondary education and training. Increasingly, researchers and policy analysts recognize that the necessary qualities for persistence in and completion of postsecondary education involve more than just academic components.[4]

In order for young people to set future goals, make informed choices, and succeed once in college, they need opportunities that support their holistic development. They need additional developmental supports that work in tandem with—not instead of—the academic, aspirational, informational, and financial supports described earlier. These strategies can include activities and interactions that set them up to build college-going identities, develop positive motivational habits and regulatory skills, and instill agency and can support many other processes that we explore in later chapters of this book.

A Limited Range of Youth Served

The majority of college access and success programs offered today focus on providing information and support to youth who are currently underrepresented in higher education, including low-income youth, first-generation college-bound students, and those from ethnic and racial minority groups. But experience and research suggest that these programs may not be reaching those young people at greatest educational risk. Several years ago, one of us was involved in a research study which found that successful first-generation college students had availed themselves of not just one but many precollege programs and supports. While suggesting that these youth had benefited from these programs, the findings were simultaneously troubling. The research team began to wonder: if the small sample of participants in this study had participated in multiple programs and received support from several caring adults, had there been any program spots or supports left for those youth who weren't as motivated or who didn't have as much initiative? Might this have explained why some of those youth never made it to college?

Some precollege and youth-serving organizations offer open access to any young person, thereby making their resources available to anyone interested in going to college. However, others require participants to meet specific criteria, such as minimum grade point averages or lengthy application processes—requirements that may weed out the very young people that adults most need to reach. And even programs that don't have such eligibility requirements tend to serve the youth most likely to succeed regardless of their participation; they possess the confidence, vision, and planning skills that make them more likely both to seek out support and to succeed in college. Further compounding the problem, practitioners often think of youth who don't knock on their office doors or who don't submit applications as unmotivated or undeserving of their time and attention. So what supports are in place for the young man or woman who does not already envision a post-

secondary future or who lacks the skills or criteria to participate in a particular enrichment program?

There is little documentation of the exact number of young
people served by current college access programs. However,
Watson Scott Swail and Laura Perna reviewed participation in
federal TRIO programs, outreach programs that target college
access support to low-income and first-generation students as
well as to students with disabilities. Swail and Perna found that
these programs serve only about 14 percent of eligible youth.[5]
And even without concrete data on what percentage of youth are
served by other programs, we can guess from college enrollment
data that current efforts are either not reaching or not working
for all youth, especially those from underrepresented groups.

There are myriad reasons why current efforts fail to reach
some youth. In the case of school counselors, high caseloads
and intense emotional needs among some students often result in an inability to reach all students. As was the case for
Mr. White, who we mentioned in the introduction, extremely
large caseloads often result in time going to those students who
are most persistent. Similarly, many community-based programs have a limited number of slots based on limited funding. Most educators and youth workers can recall a young person who was turned away from an amazing opportunity based
on too few slots. While some programs use lotteries and other
systems to promote equity, many rely on a first-come-first-
served approach. Even among those programs that struggle to
fill their slots, limited resources often prevent staff from conducting extensive recruitment. And because programs need to
focus their resources on youth who are most likely to benefit,
many postsecondary planning programs require a minimum
grade point average for entry, inherently limiting the number

of youth who can participate. Taken together, these facts seem to suggest that current efforts are not only missing out on a population of young people but are only beginning to scratch the surface in creating equitable access.

We see a developmental focus to college access work as instrumental in addressing this equity problem. Thinking about the developmental skills that youth need just to get in the door of programs or to hear the messages of supportive adults can help practitioners and policy makers target their efforts to build these skills in young people both before and during dedicated college access efforts. This perspective can also help traditional college access professionals build connections with practitioners who work in related fields and programs, such as arts and sports, and who want to expand their services to include college access and readiness.

Limited and Inconsistent Approaches to Training

College-going aspirations and behaviors are shaped by a range of significant people in youths' lives, including school personnel, parents, community members, and peers. Several years ago, one of us gathered qualitative data on graduates of urban high schools and their experiences in their first and second years of college. This study asked students, "Who and what programs helped you along your path to higher education?" Students responded with long lists of people and programs, noting that enrollment in one program often led to participation in others and provided access to several supportive mentoring relationships. The responses confirmed previous suspicions that it is often not any one program or person, but rather a constellation of programs and supports which ensure that low-income, first-generation students have the resources to achieve postsecondary success. However, one major challenge to helping youth draw on a wide range of resources is that practitioners' preservice pathways differ markedly. And practitioners from many of these pathways often lack sufficient training in adolescent development and/ or in making connections between that training and college planning and preparation.

Schools constitute the primary source of support for young people's postsecondary preparation and plans. Although there is much variation across school type, level, and mission, schools typically provide students postsecondary support through academic instruction, advisories, developmental school counseling, and college-going cultures. School counselors, who have been traditionally charged with postsecondary planning, lead classroom guidance lessons, conduct individual and group counseling sessions, and work with families to advance students' postsecondary aspirations and goals. However, school counselors, who typically hold master's degrees in counseling and licenses provided by state departments of education, rarely obtain training in college counseling; instead, their preservice training emphasizes clinical counseling skills, typically in the areas of counseling theories, career counseling, and psychological testing. In fact, according to the National Association of College Admissions Counseling, out of the more than four hundred counselor education programs in graduate schools, only about forty include a credit-bearing course specific to college counseling, and even these courses are not necessarily required.[6]

In addition to counselors, teachers and administrators have become increasingly involved in providing postsecondary supports for students. Teacher- and staff-led advisories, which use classroom settings to build relationships among teachers and students, also serve as a stage for college planning work. In addition to more traditional academic support through instruction and advanced college readiness curricula, schools also enhance college access through missions that embed high expectations and college-going norms in the culture. However, teachers and administrators have little access to training or professional development in how to support college access in ways other than traditional academic preparation. This is particularly true for the kinds of developmental processes such as identity and motivation that are most uncommon and yet clearly needed in college access efforts. In fact, a recent report commissioned by the National Council for Accreditation of Teacher Education found that few teacher preparation programs require a sufficient amount of coursework in child and adolescent development and that even fewer provide opportunities for helping students apply such coursework to practice.[7]

While schools act as the central providers of college preparation, there are a host of other organizations, programs, and institutions that enhance school and home supports. The federal government has historically provided financial and instrumental support (e.g., application completion), primarily through federal TRIO programs, including GEAR UP (Gaining Early Awareness and Readiness for Undergraduate Programs), Educational Talent Search, and Upward Bound. Outside of federal funding, community- and campus-based precollege programs provide financial aid planning, college exploration and preparation, tutoring, advising, and transition support. Staff providing these services range from college students and recent graduates to veteran higher education administrators from a range of academic backgrounds often completely outside of the education and social service realms. Practitioners who work in these types of precollege programs generally receive training on the instrumental aspects of college-going but not on adolescent development.

Youth development and afterschool programs are relatively new players in the effort to nurture and support young people's future planning. While these organizations have existed for a long time, many have recently expanded their missions to include programs and activities that support preparation and planning for college. Operating after school or during the summer, these organizations aim to help youth explore and develop career interests by providing apprenticeship and mentoring opportunities, and an increasing number are designed to build young people's interests in and paths toward careers in science, technology, engineering, and math. Because these organizations and programs have more flexibility than schools, different missions, and staff members with different training and foci, they provide unique opportunities. They are well positioned to cultivate skills that may not fit into the regular school day, to expand on skills taught during the school day in different and creative ways, and to help youth explore new interests that they may not have time for during the school day. Such opportunities have made these programs important stakeholders in closing the gaps in postsecondary access, working both on their own and in partnership with school and university staff. However, youth development practitioners have typically had few training opportunities of any kind. Although this is beginning to change, there is little opportunity for depth around adolescent development and certainly little training in college access.

This diversity of settings and professionals supporting college access is welcome, and even vital. At the same time, it poses a challenge, because the preservice pathways and in-service professional development opportunities for these varying professional roles are quite different. A deeper understanding of youth development can provide common ground for all of these diverse professionals and serve as a step toward providing a formal knowledge base for college access work across fields. Relevant topics can be integrated into preservice and in-service training programs. Doing so will better equip future practitioners to respond accordingly to the types of behaviors and belief systems that they encounter in their work. And for those educators who are already skilled in developmental theory and processes, explicit training in this area will enable them to draw the critical links to college-going behaviors.

THE TIME FOR A PARADIGM SHIFT

Applying a developmental perspective to address these challenges represents a paradigm shift in current efforts to increase young people's ability to access and succeed in college. Fortunately, we currently find ourselves with a window of opportunity for making this kind of change and for improving educational equity. Today's educational climate is ripe with conversations about the importance of educational supports for college access and success. Never before have policy makers, researchers, and practitioners engaged in this topic to such a wide degree and with such national attention. As we noted earlier, there is also a broader sense of responsibility for college access and success than ever before, with multiple settings and professionals engaged. This increased interest can be seen through national initiatives and leadership, new dimensions of education reform, the shifting of responsibility and roles in schools, and expansion of nonprofit programs and services.

Today's economic recession, which has had an especially large impact on those who do not possess college degrees, coupled with a focus from federal policy makers on the need for a knowledge-based economy, has sparked a new level of attention to postsecondary degree attainment. According to the Georgetown University Center on Education and the Workforce, by the year 2018, 63 percent of jobs will require a postsecondary credential.[8] Furthermore, postsecondary credentials have been shown to be associated with benefits to individuals (better health outcomes, increased earning potential, economic mobility, and greater life satisfaction) and to society (low unemployment rates, increased tax revenues, greater civic and volunteer participation, and less dependency on social services). In response to these trends, there has been new federal interest in the simplification of financial aid forms, large-scale investments in community colleges, protection of federal Pell Grant amounts, and new grant opportunities such as the College Access Challenge Grant.

Another indicator of growing interest is that college readiness has become integrated into education reform efforts in a more central way than ever before. Schools are increasingly using college enrollment as a marker for secondary school success. For example, anyone who has seen *Waiting for Superman*, the 2010 documentary film by director Davis Guggenheim, knows that many, if not most, of today's charter schools proclaim college enrollment as their goal. Early College High Schools give high school students the chance to enroll in college courses to simultaneously obtain high school credits and explore postsecondary options. And another noteworthy shift is the fact that elementary and middle schools are embedding expectations and preparation for college-going into their cultures, reflecting a shift away from solely associating high schools with college preparation responsibility.

A positive outcome of this widespread interest in college access and success is a shift toward mutual responsibility for supporting young people's futures—and an opportunity for working even more intentionally to build partnerships that benefit young people. This change reflects a move away from blaming individuals or organizations for their shortcomings and toward seeing the solution as multifaceted. It is critical, then, that everyone working in college access—whether in schools, afterschool and summer programs, policy, or other settings—have a shared understanding of how development influences college-going behaviors so that their efforts can complement one another.

MEETING THE CHALLENGES HEAD-ON

All of the trends described above are positive signs, which suggest that practitioners and policy makers are poised to learn from and apply a developmental perspective to their current efforts and to new efforts moving forward. The time is right to shift our perspective and rethink our strategies in order to truly increase the number of youth who aspire to, enroll in, and succeed in college. To borrow from a popular educational reform strategy, we need to *differentiate* our practices to meet students where they are and help them get to where they want to go. This will require that we refocus our energies. Does it require that we abandon current approaches? No. Does it mean changing the way we approach our work? Yes. And making this change is as much about *how* we do our work as about *what* we do.

2

BECOMING DEVELOPMENTALLY AWARE

Applying Developmental Theory to College
Preparation and Planning

D evelopment shapes everything that youth do, and it
should shape everything that adults do with and for
them, from organizational structures to daily interactions.
When I (Suzanne) conducted my graduate work in developmental and educational psychology, friends and colleagues
would sometimes ask me, "Are you a developmentalist, a cli-
nician, or a teacher?" The question always struck me as odd.
Shouldn't we all be developmentalists?

Being a developmentalist, or taking a developmental approach, simply means working with youth in a way that incorporates a big-picture understanding of their social, emotional,
and cognitive development and how it shapes their behavior. For all youth practitioners, whether they provide counseling services, run afterschool programs, or teach math, and
for those who support youth professionals by making policy

or conducting research, understanding development is an essential skill that makes it possible to recognize why youth do what they do and how they might do it differently. A middle schooler's persistence and organizational skills influence his ability to learn from the math teacher. A high schooler's hopes and self-confidence influence whether she applies to participate in a college access program, and her relationships influence whether she shares the information she receives with her family and friends. Understanding these connections provides a clearer picture of young people's needs and valuable insights about how to meet those needs.

INTEGRATION LEADS TO INSPIRATION

Making these connections and working effectively with youth requires the integration of theory, research, and practical experience. Research without practical experience can be abstract or irrelevant. Practice that isn't grounded in theory and research tends to rely on personal experience, which is necessarily limited for even the most seasoned professionals. In our work with practitioners and policy makers, we've discovered that theory sometimes gets a bad reputation. But theory, when presented in an applied manner, can be so useful that it literally changes the lives of adults, their programs, and their youth.

Raw Art Works (RAW), a youth arts nonprofit organization in Lynn, Massachusetts, has seen this transformation. In 2008, RAW launched the Boston Youth Arts Evaluation Project (BYAEP), a collaborative effort among several arts programs, funders, and researchers to create an evaluation framework designed specifically to capture the strengths and challenges of arts programs.[1] For RAW, what began as an effort to create an evaluation tool became a new way of approaching daily work with youth. The BYAEP team conducted a detailed review of youth development theories, followed by an intensive process of exploring how these theories matched up with the work that RAW and their partner organizations were doing with adolescents. The result was the creation of a new framework which has three categories that capture the goals and strengths of arts programs and encompass developmental theories and skills: "I Am" includes processes such as identity and motivation; "I Create" includes engagement, problem solving, and skill development; and "We Connect" includes strong relationships and a sense of belonging. The BYAEP team has created evaluation tools based on these categories, but RAW and others have applied the framework much more broadly, in a way that is transforming their organizations and, they hope, the lives of their youth participants. RAW now uses the developmental framework and its three categories to help all youth and all employees of RAW to set their own goals for what they hope they will accomplish, to create new programming tailored to adolescents' developmental needs, and to assess how participating youth and the programs that serve them are progressing in each of the categories.

RAW has learned something that is important for everyone who works with youth: it is vital to recognize and reflect on the perspectives that each person brings to the work, especially the perspectives that they may be missing. Consciously or not, everyone has certain perspectives that are shaped by individual lived experience, training, informal education, values, beliefs, and experiences. For example, as we began writing this book, we discovered that our knowledge and strategies shared common ground but also reflected our unique backgrounds. In many ways, practitioners' uniqueness enables them to bring passion and insight to their work. However, it is all too easy for personal experiences and current perspectives to become entrenched. In fact, research from social psychology shows that people tend to look for and pay more attention to information that confirms their previously held beliefs. This means that, without realizing it, professionals from many backgrounds and in many roles may be putting on blinders that limit their vision and ability to take in important information.

Fortunately, theory and research can help to remove these unintentional blinders, because they provide additional knowledge that broadens and builds on personal experience. This is particularly important for working with youth from a broad and diverse set of backgrounds. Even those who have worked in their fields for many years and been exposed to many different contexts and experiences cannot hope to have personal experience with the full range of backgrounds, perspectives, and needs of all youth. This reality is highlighted by the fact that many practitioners come from different cultural, ethnic, linguistic, and socioeconomic backgrounds than the young people with whom they work. Cultural influences, identities, and perspectives play important roles in many stages of the college-going process, from influencing the formation of a college-going identity to shaping choices about whether to attend college, where to apply, and what to study. As we have seen in our work, relying strictly on one's own personal experience with the college-going process, or even on past experience with youth in the same schools and communities, may get in the way of addressing these factors adequately. For example, motivation to attend college can come from multiple sources. For some youth, motivation is derived from topical interests or career goals, while for others it is economically driven or even personal. These varying forms of motivation mean that adults cannot use their personal drives and assume that they will apply to all youth.

Because they provide a broader perspective, research and theory can inspire creativity (not stifle it, as some assume). They can help practitioners to look for and find youths' personal stories and to be reflective and thoughtful about those stories. They can then help practitioners and leaders develop their own strategies that are differentiated and tailored to meet young people's individual backgrounds, needs, strengths, and challenges.

Three core principles derived from research and theory provide a foundation for understanding how specific developmental processes relate to college access and success. First, developmental stages matter and should inform how adults approach their work with youth. Adolescence plays an especially important role in college-going and is the focus of many college access programs and policies. Second, young people can and should be active agents in the college process. Despite many college access efforts that view adolescents as immature and/or passive recipients of services, research shows that adolescents have a wealth of assets and the capability to leverage those assets to construct positive futures for themselves—if they are provided with the necessary supports and opportunities. Third, college-going is an interconnected process that is shaped by and in turn shapes young people's social, emotional, and cognitive development as well as their social contexts, including families, peers, schools, and communities.

DEVELOPMENTAL STAGES MATTER

There is a reason why classrooms are structured differently for preschoolers and fifth-graders and why professors have different expectations for incoming college freshmen and graduating seniors: developmental stages matter. While it is helpful for professionals who work with youth to have a broad understanding of development over time, it is essential to have a clear understanding of their students' current developmental stage and of those immediately preceding and following it. This is necessary to ensure that strategies and practices are focused and effective.

There is no doubt that college access and success begin early in a child's life. Through family expectations and aspirations, academic support and preparation, and other avenues, children begin to form identities, habits, and academic trajectories in elementary school or even earlier. The developmental processes that shape college-going do not begin or end in adolescence. As generations of theorists and researchers such as Erik Erikson (whose theories we describe in chapter 3) have pointed out, developmental stages build on one another and are best understood within long-term trajectories. But college-going consumes an increasing amount of time and attention during middle school and high school, and most of the professionals who dedicate their efforts to college access work at these grade levels. (Of course, there can be significant differences among those at the younger and older ends of this wide age range, and throughout this book we note these differences where they have implications for college access strategies and approaches.)

While college access occurs before and during adolescence, college success is attained during a subsequent developmental stage that psychologist Jeffrey Arnett refers to as *emerging adulthood*. According to Arnett, emerging adulthood is a relatively new phenomenon and is unique to certain parts of the world "in which young people are allowed to postpone entering adult roles such as marriage and parenthood until at least their mid 20's."[2] These tend to be in industrialized countries and in societies where young people have the opportunity to make choices about their futures. Arnett distinguishes emerging adulthood from the stages that precede and follow it (adolescence and adulthood) based on a set of unique tasks and characteristics that are focused on establishing oneself in the domains of work and love. These include the experience of instability in work and relationships, common feelings of being "in-between" and in transition, exploring multiple roles and identities, and feeling a sense of possibility in the face of an open future. Some of these feelings and experiences are the continuation of processes begun during adolescence, while others arise during the late teens and twenties.

YOUTH ARE ACTIVE AGENTS IN THE COLLEGE-GOING PROCESS

Many current beliefs and practices in education and youth work are influenced by historical notions of adolescent development. In the early 1900s, G. Stanley Hall introduced the description of adolescence as a time of "storm and stress." This focus on conflict and confusion gave rise to a tenacious view of adolescents as "problems to be managed" and to almost a century's worth of efforts to address adolescents' risks and problems. Psychologist Robert Epstein believes that this negative focus is detrimental and that it has actually been a *cause* of the problems that we see among some adolescents.[3] Epstein suggests that our culture has artificially and inappropriately extended childhood beyond puberty, providing freedom in certain ways (especially socially) while providing few opportunities for real responsibility. The result, he believes, is an "infantilizing" effect on how our society treats adolescents. He points out that the number of laws restricting adolescents' behaviors has increased since the 1960s and is currently ten times higher than those for adults, and twice as high as those for incarcerated felons. And as psychologist Reed Larson, who has spent years studying youth beliefs and behaviors, has pointed out, middle schools offer few opportunities for student choice and initiative at an age when these opportunities are most needed and most developmentally appropriate.[4]

We believe that the widespread focus on adolescent problems and the lack of attention to assets has influenced college access efforts and is one reason for a trend in removing young people's agency from the process. Unfortunately, it has been common to view college preparation as something that is done *to* and *for* young people rather than *with* them as active contributors. This perspective is in striking contrast to a growing movement in research and youth work practice over the last two decades that focuses on leveraging adolescents' strengths, building their resilience, and helping them be active and responsible agents in their own lives. To be sure, adolescents navigate many stressful tasks and transitions, including social, academic, and biological changes, and many first-generation college students experience additional stressors associated with having low family income, balancing family and work obligations, and navigating a process with which their families have no experience—stresses that heavily influence the processes of applying to, preparing for, and succeeding in college. But research shows what many of us who work with youth have known all along: adolescents are capable and creative people with broad strengths, deep resilience, and much to contribute to their families, schools, and communities.

This insight is reflected in the positive youth development (PYD) perspective, which emerged in the early 1990s and has increasingly informed programs that serve children and adolescents. PYD shifts focus away from ameliorating risks and negative outcomes and toward promoting positive outcomes and contributions to self, family, school, community, and society. PYD emerged in response to several trends, including growing knowledge about the plasticity of the brain and the capacity for development across the lifespan, the role of social environments in shaping development, and the birth of the positive psychology movement. Guided by this foundation, PYD views youth in a way described by the now-popular phrase "assets to be developed rather than problems to be managed." Indeed, adolescents have tremendous potential and internal resources, and many even demonstrate impressive resilience in the face of very difficult challenges, such as living in poverty and experiencing family trauma. Consistent with this focus on assets, PYD highlights the fact that succeeding in life requires the development of skills and positive adjustment. In the words of Forum for Youth Investment president Karen Pittman, "problem free is not fully prepared."[5] This is something that counselors and other youth workers know well, because college admissions require more than a problem-free disciplinary record, and the social and academic challenges of college require focused preparation and internal resources such as motivation and self-regulation.

The PYD perspective has pointed out not only that adolescents are capable of great things but also that adults need to provide more opportunities for them to accomplish those things, especially because many of them are not currently realizing their full potential. For example, the 4-H Study of Positive Youth Development, a longitudinal study of more than six thousand youth in forty-five states, found that over 75 percent of youth in fifth through tenth grades manifested no specific problems or risky behaviors and that the majority make positive contributions to their schools, families, and communities. But the study also found that only about 9 percent of youth made the highest possible levels of these kinds of contributions.[6] We have seen similar discrepancies in college access and success. Take, for example, the case of Victor, a high-achieving high school senior in a low-achieving urban high school. When asked by one of his biggest supporters, a high school arts teacher, about his college plans, Victor replied that he was planning to attend the local community college. His teacher, aware of his good grades in AP classes, strong work ethic, and role as a student leader, provided him with information about local universities and about his eligibility for financial aid and repeatedly inquired about his decision not to attend a more competitive school. Victor's shrugs and "I dunnos" consistently suggested that he lacked either the confidence or motivation to pursue such opportunities. Researchers Caroline Hoxby and Christopher Avery have referred to this type of behavior as *undermatching*, the process in which qualified low-income youth apply to fewer and less selective colleges than their more affluent peers with similar academic credentials.[7]

PYD also highlights the need for another shift in college access and success efforts: youth need to take an active role in shaping and walking their own paths. As educators and parents know, adolescents have a strong need—and a powerful determination—to make their own choices and to act independently. For many youth, college is the beginning of their own independently chosen and directed paths. But few institutions and efforts have harnessed this need to build agency, or what Reed Larson has described as *initiative*, "the ability to be motivated from within to direct attention and effort toward a challenging goal."[8] According to Larson, initiative or "agency" involves three factors that work in concert: *intrinsic motivation*, or the drive to do something and invest in it for its own sake; *engagement* in the activities and environments of one's daily life; and *commitment* over time even (or especially) in the face of challenges and setbacks. Initiative is not an inborn trait but, rather, develops within youths' daily lives as a result of strong and effective relationships with adults and peers, opportunities to explore interests and develop skills, and chances for autonomy and responsibility. Larson's research shows that many, if not most, of the settings where youth spend their time have one or two of these characteristics but not all three; therefore, they do not promote the development of initiative. In fact, his study of adolescents' time use and emotional states found that participants reported feeling bored a surprising 27 percent of the time, suggesting that there is plenty of room for improvement in motivation and engagement. We believe that if a study like Larson's looked at college access programs and practices, it would find a similar lack of attention to many of the components of agency. We also believe that incorporating the development of agency into existing programs is as doable as it is important.

Whereas PYD has yet to be incorporated into most college access and success efforts, it has had a major impact on many other youth-focused fields, including those that can influence college access and success. For example, it has been a major contributor to changes in the field of afterschool programs over the past twenty years. While afterschool programs have been in place since the turn of the century, they grew in number and scope in the 1970s and 1980s. This growth was due largely to an increase in maternal employment, which led programs and policies to frame them as "school-aged child care," with a focus on keeping youth safe and supervised while their parents worked. However, with the emergence of PYD in the early 1990s (along with other factors, including calls for more attention to academics), the focus of structured afterschool programs shifted to an emphasis on providing opportunities for youth to develop interests and skills, to contribute to their communities, and to shape their futures, including postsecondary education. (In fact, helping prepare youth for college and postsecondary careers—especially in science, technology, engineering, and math (STEM)—has become a common focus in many afterschool programs.) The result of this shift is that thousands of children and youth (as many as 8 million in grades K–12, according to the advocacy organization the Afterschool Alliance) now have more opportunities to reach their current and future potential than they did a few decades ago.[9]

PYD has the potential to transform college access efforts in the same way that it has influenced afterschool programming, and national data underscore the need for this transformation. As described in chapter 1, despite increasing enrollment, large numbers of young people are not pursuing postsecondary education, especially among youth who are from low-income families, ethnic minorities, and first-generation college-bound students. So if young people are competent, capable, and relatively problem free, why aren't more of them on positive postsecondary paths? Why do adolescent development experts like Larson find that "many youth do their schoolwork, comply with their parents, hang out with their friends, and get through the day, but are not invested in paths into the future that excite them or feel like they originate from within"?[10]

One of the reasons is that they need appropriate and effective scaffolding. The term *scaffolding* was popularized by Lev Vygotsky, a Russian psychologist working in the early 1900s. According to Vygotsky, education should target a child's *zone of proximal development*—that is, the area between what a child can do on his or her own and what he or she can do with assistance from helpful, engaged others, including adults and peers. This assistance is most effective when it is provided as scaffolding: assistance that provides just enough support to help the young person learn how to do the task herself. Educators who are skillful gradually reduce the amount of scaffolding for each task over time while they begin providing scaffolding for the next set of developing skills. In order for adults to scaffold successfully, they need a clear understanding of development, including when certain skills emerge and how they mature over time. This approach is evident in college preparation curricula that take a staged approach, beginning with exploration of self ("Who am I? What do I want to be?") and then moving to planning ("How do I get there from here?" "What degree is required for that career?").

COLLEGE-GOING IS AN INTERCONNECTED PROCESS

College-going does not happen in a vacuum. A young person's postsecondary path is shaped by many people, practices, experiences, and programs, and is also intimately connected to the many developmental processes occurring within that young person's life. In other words, college-going is an interconnected process shaped by both external and internal connections. This may seem like common sense; in education and youth work today, it is commonplace to acknowledge the role of youths' families, friends, communities, and cultures. This wasn't always the case, however.

Early psychoanalytic and other psychological theories placed a nearly exclusive focus on mother-child relationships, which carried over to many child- and adolescent-serving fields. In the 1970s, Urie Bronfenbrenner initiated a major shift in thinking with his ecological systems theory, which described individuals as embedded within a series of systems or levels of influence. Bronfenbrenner gave each of these levels a label, but the labels are not as important as the overall themes of the theory. One of these themes is that we are all shaped by our environments (including not just our immediate families but also our peers), by institutions with which we interact (such as schools and neighborhoods), by institutions with which significant others in our lives interact (e.g., parents' workplaces), by wider cultural and political influences, and by the historical periods in which we live. A second theme is that these levels all interact with one another, and a third is that the interactions between individuals and these other levels of influence are multidirectional. For example, individual students can and do shape school cultures and norms, and school cultures in turn influence individual students, creating ongoing feedback loops.

In the decades since Bronfenbrenner introduced ecological systems theory, he and others have proposed more complex and nuanced models of the ways in which individuals and their many social contexts interact. Whether these theories are called developmental ecological models, transactional models, or person-in-environment models, the take-home message is the same: context matters. This message is good news for educators and others who work with youth, because it means that what we do has enormous potential to shape youths' lives. When it comes to college access, we have the opportunity to be open-minded and creative about where, when, and with whom preparation and support processes occur. School counselors play an essential role in youths' postsecondary aspirations and plans. But many other professionals and institutions can and do support college access and success, including out-of-school time programs, community institutions, arts and recreation centers, and formal and informal mentors. Each of these settings matters, and practitioners in each can incorporate youth development research and theory to support college-going behaviors. Furthermore, all of these practitioners have the potential to reinforce and leverage one another's efforts.

Just as the college-going process is influenced by youths' social settings, it is also connected with and influenced by other developmental processes. As adolescents prepare for their postsecondary lives, they are also experiencing major biological shifts (e.g., hormonal and neurological), exploring their identities, and experimenting with new social challenges and opportunities in everything from paid employment to driving to substance use. All of these facets of development—biological, cognitive, social, emotional—are interconnected in ways that psychologists have recently begun referring to as *developmental cascades*. Like a cascading waterfall, development of one skill or domain flows into and through others, feeding a constant cycle in which there is no clear beginning or end.

Cascade theory has shaped our thinking by pointing out three important points about development. First, skills in one domain influence the development of skills in other domains. One of the most well-documented examples of this is in the integral relationship between social and emotional skills and academic achievement. Interpersonal skills influence academic performance by shaping a young student's ability to work in groups, follow directions, and get along with the teacher. Intrapersonal skills also influence achievement; for example, a young person's self-efficacy, or belief that she can accomplish a goal, shapes her effort and therefore her achievement. Because high school achievement is so important for college, it's easy to see a developmental cascade from social and emotional skills to achievement to college access and success.

Second, there are connections among an individual's behaviors and those of her peers, family members, school, and other social institutions. In fact, research shows that one student's behavior can influence a whole classroom or peer group dynamic, and vice versa. One student who acts out in class can distract the teacher, disrupting her ability to teach effectively, and also other students, making it difficult for them to focus or affecting their beliefs about the "cool" or acceptable ways of acting in class. As we describe in chapter 7, we believe that these peer dynamics can also influence—not only for worse, but for better—whether a young person adopts a college-going identity and thus applies to and graduates from college.

Third, development occurs over time, with each new stage building on those that came before it. This principle is easy to see in academic development; you can't learn algebra without learning basic arithmetic. But it also applies to many other developmental processes, such as the development of self-regulation.

Self-regulation—the ability to manage one's thoughts, emotions, and behaviors and to marshal them in support of a goal—is essential to college access, because applying to and succeeding in college requires the ability to set both short- and long-term goals, to plan and organize in support of those goals, and to persist in the face of challenges. The fact that developmental tasks and skills build on one another over time is why it is so important to lay the academic, social, and other foundations for college-going early in life, and why it is so important for those working with adolescents to understand their students' past, present, and future development as it relates to college-going. It is also one of the reasons that it is important to provide developmentally appropriate scaffolding of the kind that Vygotsky described.

Developmental cascades occur naturally as youth grow and develop, but they can also be initiated or shaped through programs and practices. Programs that aim to create positive cascades are typically designed to effect changes in desired outcomes by targeting a series of intermediate steps. For example, programs that have the ultimate goal of preventing bullying and violence among youth often target young people's empathy, perspective taking, and social skills, which make them more likely to be respectful and tolerant and less likely to engage in harassment or other hurtful behaviors. This has become the norm in prevention science, a field that aims to prevent risky behaviors and promote positive ones in youth. However, this wasn't always the case. Early generations of prevention programs were well-intentioned and sometimes even well-resourced, but they tended to have few significant effects, largely because they did not apply the science of youth development to understand why and how the targeted problems—and the programs to prevent them—worked. Fortunately, researchers used these early programs to learn more about the role of youth development, especially in effecting intermediate changes. Later generations of programs incorporated this knowledge to target intermediate steps in order to reach their ultimate outcomes. This approach has proven highly successful in prevention science, and evaluations have shown many of these programs to be significantly effective.

The successful application of research on youth development in prevention science and other fields has much to teach college access and success efforts. One of the lessons it offers is a focus on understanding not just *what* youth do, but *why* and *how*. In today's data-driven world, education is often compared to the field of medicine: just as doctors need data about what treatments work and for whom, those who work with youth need to know what prevention and intervention strategies work best for whom and under what circumstances. But doctors and youth workers also need to know about the why and how. Doctors need behavioral health research to understand why their patients do or don't take the medications prescribed or engage in the recommended lifestyle changes; without this kind of research, they would be left scratching their heads and wondering, "Why doesn't she take her medication and exercise regularly even though I told her that it would help prevent a heart attack?" Similarly, professionals who work with adolescents need to understand why youth do or don't take advantage of and benefit from preparation and support services; missing this information, too many professionals are left scratching their heads and wondering, "Why hasn't he applied to college even though I helped him register for all the right courses and fill out the FAFSA?"

In the chapters that follow, we describe the roles of identity, motivation, self-regulation, and relationships in college access and success, and how understanding these processes can help answer such questions. We provide strategies for leveraging these processes in positive ways and examples of how we and our colleagues have used them. But our main goal is to help practitioners think differently about their work with and for youth—to help all practitioners to become developmentalists.

PART II

Changing the Approach

3

ENVISIONING

Forming an Identity That Includes
College-Going

S everal years ago, one of us ran a college awareness program at a local university for ninth-graders from an inner-
city high school. The eight-week program required youth to
show up at 9:00 in the morning for a four-hour program called
Saturday Explorations. At the start of every semester, one of
the biggest questions facing the program staff was, "Will thirty
fourteen- and fifteen-year-olds be willing to take a bus across
the city on a Saturday morning to learn about going to college?" So each semester it came as a pleasant surprise that the
program had more applicants than available slots. But what
didn't come as a surprise was that most, if not all, of the applications came from youth who already viewed themselves as
people who belonged in, were capable of, and were headed for
college—those who already possessed a college-going identity.
Recruiting youth who didn't already see "college-goer" as part

of their identity was one of the major challenges in that program, and it is one of the biggest and most important challenges in promoting equity in college access and success.

When we ask college counselors and other youth professionals about the most important element in helping young people get to and succeed in college, many of them mention something about instilling a college-going identity. We see this theme repeated in the mission statements of many college access programs. Most of these practitioners and programs use the term *college-going identity* to describe the state of mind in which youth believe that college is right for them, see themselves as "college material," and aspire to obtain a college degree. Typically, their efforts to instill a college-going identity focus on raising educational aspirations and exposing youth to an array of postsecondary awareness and readiness activities. These efforts are certainly valuable. But they are missing a crucial component: the "identity" part of "college-going identity."

During adolescence, young people are constantly asking questions such as "Who am I?" "Where do I fit in?" "What do I want to do with my life?" These questions, and their ever-evolving answers, shape everything that young people do. How young people come to see themselves as individuals, as members of certain groups, and as people who fill certain roles influence whether they see themselves as "college material" and inform the working narratives that they hold of themselves as college-goers. In turn, this shapes whether they set college-going goals, seek mentors, and sign up for programs like Saturday Explorations. It also influences whether they remain committed to college-going even when obstacles present themselves. Understanding the larger processes of identity development is therefore critical for college access efforts. In fact, it may be one of the most significant hurdles to overcoming gaps in college access and success, because identity is the foundation on which many other behaviors are based. Yet, this process of identity development goes unnoticed by most practitioners.

In our work, we have seen few examples of strategies that intentionally target the processes of identity development. We have also seen many missed opportunities to enhance existing practices by more intentionally addressing the role of identity development. Our goal here is to shine light on and demystify the concept of identity and the specific salience it has for adolescents in developing a college-going identity. We describe not only how identity development matters but how practitioners can support it.

In this chapter, you will learn:

- Why identity development is central for adolescents
- Why it is important to support adolescents' identity explorations, even if they appear inconsistent with college-going
- How to prevent young people from prematurely deciding against college
- How to help youth navigate identity conflicts
- How to support identity development by engaging young people in reflective dialogue

ADOLESCENTS AS EXPLORERS

Identity development—the process of exploring and understanding who one is both as a unique individual and as a member of certain groups—is an ever-evolving process, but one that is particularly central during adolescence. In fact, it is probably the most important developmental task of this period. One of the first people to clearly articulate this was Eric Erikson, who argued that individuals pass through a series of eight psychological stages across development, each of which is driven by a task or "crisis" that needs to be successfully navigated before the individual can move into the next developmental stage. For example, in early childhood, infants must develop a secure attachment to one or more primary caregivers so that they feel secure enough to explore the world around them and then move on to developing some autonomy. Assuming that they successfully navigate the first four stages, adolescents usually find themselves in the stage that Erikson referred to as "fidelity: identity versus role confusion."[1] The central goal of this stage is the formation of a coherent identity that merges past and present experiences. During this stage of development, youth begin to make sense of who they are and where they are going with their lives in the context of the multiple dimensions of their identity. Resolving this identity "crisis" lays the foundation for the subsequent stages of middle adulthood and is therefore essential for developing a successful future.

Erikson's theory has several important implications for college access efforts, two of which are worth mentioning at the outset of our discussion of identity. First, it points out that identity development is a process. Because no one progresses through this process at the exact same rate, youth fall along a continuum of exploring identity in general and college-going identity in particular. Some of them have already made a clear commitment to being college-goers, while others are just beginning to explore this potential part of their identity. But too many college access programs only serve youth who already see themselves as college-goers. For example, many college access efforts use grade point averages and other eligibility requirements that restrict participation to those youth who have already begun to form college-going identities. Ironically, these programs provide the kinds of exploratory and preparatory opportunities that would help other youth begin to see themselves as college-goers. There is a clear need for programs and services designed for youth who do not already embody a college-going identity and who may therefore not be living up to their academic potential or planning for their futures.

Secondly, Erikson's work reminds us that when we set out to help youth build college-going identities, we meet them in the midst of a critical developmental transition. Young people are constantly experimenting and trying on new identities, partly to determine whether those identities feel like a good match and whether they will be accepted by peers, family members, and authority figures. They explore identities through their dress or other aspects of their appearance, through new friendships and peer groups, through exploration of new activities and hobbies, and sometimes through risky behaviors that test the boundaries of laws, rules, and their own physical limitations. Young people interpret and draw meaning from these exploratory experiences as well as from experiences over which they do not have control or choice, including how others perceive them and treat them. Through this challenging but vital process, youth begin to make meaning and unify multiple dimensions of themselves in order to figure out who they are and what goals they have for themselves. All of these experiences are normal and healthy. And all of them, directly or indirectly, can have relevance for college-going.

The job of educators and other adults is to meet youth where they are in this process and to provide opportunities for exploration and reflection. One of the roles of practitioners is to help young people explore postsecondary options and understand how these options are or are not consistent with how they see themselves in the present and the future. But another important, and often overlooked, task is to allow youth to explore their broader identities and make connections between who they are and who they hope to be in the future. This is important even—or especially—when they engage in behaviors that seem like they are inconsistent with college-going. The case of Savannah illustrates this behavior.

In ninth grade, Savannah began participating in a community-based afterschool and summer program that provided tutoring support and athletic opportunities. She, along with two of her friends, joined the program because they loved sports and appreciated the kind and supportive staff who helped them with their homework. Savannah soon discovered that she also really enjoyed talking with the college student volunteers and learning about the kinds of courses and internships they were doing, especially those related to law. Savannah and her friends stuck with the program through tenth grade; however, the following summer two of Savannah's friends found jobs at the local mall and quit the program.

Savannah knew that the summer program would offer visits to local colleges and information about how to apply, along with other things that she was looking forward to. However, she also liked the idea of having a job and earning money. On top of that, she liked the idea of being "one of the girls," as her friends put it.

When her friend Lina told Savannah that the store where she worked was hiring, Savannah wavered. Lina continued to en-

courage Savannah to take the job, pointing out how much fun it would be to share shifts and adding, "You're the one who always makes time for friends. Plus, it's a customer service job, and you're so great with people—you'd be perfect!" After thinking it over, Savannah decided that her role as a leader in her peer group was important to her, and she told the supervisor of the program that she was going to take the job.

Frustrated by this decision, the program supervisor told Savannah that the summer component was required and that if she left, she would be leaving the program. Although Savannah felt bad about this, she joined her friends at the mall and accepted the fact that she could not return to the program.

While the program director's response was understandable, it resulted in a missed opportunity to continue to engage Savannah. If he had realized how important Savannah's friends were to her identity, he could have helped her find a compromise, such as allowing her to remain connected to the program while also working part time. He could also have helped her draw connections between her current identity and her future— for example, how her view of herself as a social person and a good friend might help her choose a career path in a human relations or human services field. Instead, he did what many practitioners do: when he saw Savannah behave in a way that was not consistent with adults' ideas of what dedicated youth do, he assumed that she did not want or deserve his help. Firm requirements and policies like this program's are in the spirit of high expectations, but sometimes they lead practitioners to show youth the door during the very moments when adults could support and leverage identity development.

COMMITTING TO A
COLLEGE-GOING IDENTITY

Supporting adolescents' broad identity development is an important foundation (but not substitute) for explicit conversations about whether and how young people see themselves as college-goers. While many practitioners make efforts to start these conversations, they often do not realize that college-going identity, like identity more broadly, is a process. Young people of the same age and in the same settings vary widely in where they are in this process. James Marcia, who built on the identity stage of Erikson's theory, proposed and researched a theory that provides a helpful starting place for identifying where young people are and how to best support them. In his identity status theory, Marcia describes four "statuses" that indicate the degree to which a person has explored and committed to a particular element of identity. These four statuses can aptly be applied to the process of developing a college-going identity:

- *Identity diffused* describes the individual who has not yet confronted the task of resolving his identity and as such may be confused. This student has little awareness of future postsecondary options and mostly feels overwhelmed by the process.
- *Foreclosure* refers to the state of an individual who has prematurely made a decision about an aspect of identity without a full exploration. This student has ruled out going to college without seeking or receiving appropriate information.
- *Moratorium* refers to the time when individuals are actively exploring aspects of identity and working toward

a unifying sense of self. This student is trying on the possibility of going to college but has not yet made a full commitment.

- *Identity achieved* describes the point at which an individual has fully explored his identity options and made a commitment to a particular element of identity. This student has talked with teachers, counselors, family, and/or peers and sees herself as firmly on the path to college.

In an ideal world, most high school students would fall into the moratorium status and benefit from the myriad exploratory opportunities available. Unfortunately, this is not the reality. Many young people, especially those living with economic stress and other barriers to higher education, have prematurely foreclosed on college, and others are so engrossed in the frenetic lifestyle of teenagers that they are in an identity diffused state. As a result, the challenge for practitioners is to determine which status each young person falls into and then tailor college access efforts accordingly. This differentiated approach reflects a shift from the more common approach of structuring programs only for those youth who are in the moratorium status. Using a more differentiated approach, the best use of time and resources with a young person who is in the identity diffused state would be trying to understand why he feels so overwhelmed by the college planning process rather than encouraging him to explore college campuses and majors. In contrast, when working with a young person who has foreclosed on going to college, an appropriate strategy might be to understand what has led him to this decision in order to assess what kinds of supports he needs and whether adults should and can challenge this decision. For example, a young person who has ruled out going to college because of perceptions of affordability would benefit from hearing about how federal student aid operates. But if a young person has foreclosed on college because he is very interested in a career in carpentry, then it might be better to help him find appropriate training and apprenticeship programs.

Although each status has important implications, foreclosure may be the most important one for reaching the young people who most need support: those who do not seek out opportunities such as the Saturday Explorations program. Some youth rule out the possibility of going to college because it allows them to avoid the stress that accompanies exploration and experimentation, but they also miss the benefits that come from that exploration, in this case the learning and other benefits offered by higher education. Foreclosure can occur when youth decline to experiment with the kinds of opportunities that provide positive reinforcement, receive misinformation, or experience success with an alternative (e.g., low-wage work) without fully exploring other options. This can be the result of indecisiveness, low confidence, or a fear of commitment. Because these factors operate in different ways for everyone, it is important for practitioners to consider each young person as an individual. Simply considering the possibility of premature foreclosure and aiming to prevent it is an important shift in approach from what typically occurs in schools and communities.

IDENTITY DIMENSIONS AND IDENTITY CONFLICTS

Where youth are in terms of their commitments to future goals and whether or not they are receptive to a particular type of support are influenced by many facets of their identity.

Everyone—from adolescents in the college application process to adults nearing and past retirement—has multiple dimensions to their identities. These dimensions are not all equal. Some are inherited at birth, while others are chosen. Some are most conscious when the individual is at work, others are most conscious when with friends. Some are more influential than others, but all of them influence behavior, including whether young people pursue college.

The process through which identity shapes behavior is a largely subconscious one. It works through the meaning that people make of the various dimensions of their identity and whether they associate those dimensions with college-going. If a young person sees dimensions of her identity (e.g., Latina, a high-achieving student, a devoted sister) as things that line up with going to college, then she will be more likely to envision herself as a college-goer and therefore to pursue higher education. This is a highly individual process. Two young people can claim the same element of identity (e.g., immigrant), but one may see this as consistent with college-going whereas the other sees it as inconsistent. This is because it is not the trait itself that shapes college-going but the individual's understanding of it.

Consider the following two hypothetical students. One is Hector, whose family emigrated from Ecuador when he was nine. Hector has always perceived not being born in the United States as meaning he couldn't go to college. No one has ever said this to him explicitly, although he has heard other students talking about how immigrants can't go to college. The other is Samuel, whose family recently arrived from Haiti. Samuel has long known that his parents' decision to leave family and friends in Haiti was based partially on a desire to help him find college opportunities in the United States. In both cases, these young men strongly identify as members of immigrant groups, yet one saw this as being consistent with college-going while the other saw it as inconsistent. It is not the immigration status itself but the way that the two youth understand it and interpret whether it is consistent with going to college. These meanings and interpretations, which are shaped by both overt and subtle messages in the social environment, ultimately inform what are sometimes called working narratives, or internal stories that youth tell to themselves about themselves as college-goers.

The fact that messages from the social environment shape these working narratives is important because it means that adults have a role to play in helping youth interpret and make meaning of their identities. A major goal of practitioners' work should be to provide opportunities for youth to reflect on how the various dimensions of their identities are or can be consistent with college-going, even if they do not initially see them that way. When a young person says that he does not want to go to college, it is entirely plausible that even he cannot articulate where that choice originated. By engaging him in thoughtful discussions that include questions about how he sees himself, the adults around him can help him better understand and assess his choices. Without asking questions about identity and really listening to the answers, the adults may make false assumptions; sometimes the default reaction is to assume that that young person doesn't think he's smart enough or that his socioeconomic status is in conflict with college attendance. Because identity development is such an individual process, this kind of reflective conversation is essential.

In these conversations, it is crucial to recognize that a college-going identity is not one single thing or does not look the same for all young people. For some youth, being college-goers means attending four-year universities on a full-time basis; for others, it means attending a community college or taking night classes on a part-time basis. These different types of college-going identities reflect the different goals, needs, and life situations of individual youth. But often when adults talk about and design strategies to help youth develop a college-going identity, the implicit assumption is that there is a singular version of this identity that young people must have in order to be on a successful path to college. The result is that some youth may be turned off by the well-intentioned strategies that are designed to help them. One of us remembers a young man who was determined to go to college but came to resent college visits that emphasized the social opportunities because he intended to attend on a part-time basis while working to support his family. This illustrates how when practitioners only see one version of a college-going identity, that version is often based on an upper-class version of college-going in which young people attend classes full time, live on campus, and experience college as both an academic and social experience. The unfortunate consequence is that young people who do, or could, envision other kinds of college-going paths sometimes come to believe that college is not for them. When practitioners shift their understanding to recognize multiple kinds of college-going identities, they can make a paradigm shift that allows more youth to incorporate college-going into their visions of themselves in the present and the future.

Understanding the Self in Relation to Others

Asking young people the kinds of questions that will produce fruitful dialogue requires being alert to the specific dimensions of identity that tend to influence college-going. One of the most prominent facets of identity is what social psychologist Henri Tajfel calls *social identity*.[2] According to Tajfel, people derive meaning about themselves and about their places in the world from what they believe to be true about the groups in which they are members. These conscious or unconscious beliefs shape choices and behaviors and, ultimately, other aspects of identity. This process can have positive or negative consequences for college-going because young people assess whether college is consistent with the values and behaviors of the gender, racial, religious, and other groups they identify with and behave in ways that they see as consistent with those identities.

One of the ways that social identity operates is through whether youth believe that "people like me" go to college. There are many reasons that young people may believe that "people like me" don't go to college. One of the reasons is that they simply don't see many members of the groups with which they identify (based on race, social class, neighborhood) going to college. For example, a white adolescent who sees many members of her ethnic group attending college may be more likely to believe that college is something consistent with her identity than a Native American youth who sees fewer of her peers going to college. Unfortunately, we have sometimes seen these beliefs become unintentionally reinforced in the very situations that were intended to help young people envision college-going futures for themselves. This was the case for a first-generation college-bound African American woman with whom one of us worked. This young woman had her heart set on a particular college, but after a campus visit she suddenly and clearly became convinced that the school was not a good fit for her. It took two follow-up conversations and much prodding to ultimately learn that the reason she was no longer interested was because she saw very few African American students on the campus. In this case, the experience discouraged the young woman from applying to that particular college, but similar processes could deter young people from applying to college in general, particularly if they have few other opportunities to see members of their ethnic, income, or other groups attending college.

Another reason that some young people believe that college is inconsistent with their group-based identities is that they hear people say things that suggest or reinforce the belief that people who look, sound, learn, or live they way that they do can't or don't go to college. One of us worked with a young woman named Kamilah, who assumed that her enrollment in a special education program meant that she couldn't go to college. This was partially shaped by the fact that she heard adults say derogatory things about students in special education that suggested it was impossible for them to get into or succeed in college. Unfortunately, Kamilah's beliefs about what "special ed kids" (as she referred to herself) do led her to foreclose on college. This didn't have to be the case. Kamilah was a bright, dedicated student who could have succeeded in college with appropriate supports to accommodate her learning disability. But for Kamilah to get to college, the adults around her would have needed to help her understand that enrollment in a special education program was not inconsistent with college-going.

Other reasons that young people assume that "people like me" can't go to college include lack of financial resources and immigration status. Indeed, structural barriers are very real for many young people. Many practitioners are aware of this, and, as a result, they focus on providing information about the kind of financial and other supports that are available. But what many practitioners may not realize is that these beliefs about what is possible (or perceptions of the opportunity structure) influence young people in very deep ways, right down to the fundamental identity questions of "Who am I?" and "Who can I be in the future?" These beliefs make some young people conclude, "I am not 'college material.'" These processes can start early and be deeply entrenched, so that young people may not even be aware they are occurring. As a result, many young people foreclose on the possibility of college at early ages and develop an image of the self as a non-college-goer even before adults have the chance to tell them about financial aid and other supports that may be available to them.

Youth from low-income families are particularly vulnerable to this premature foreclosure, as are undocumented youth, or students who are not legal residents of the United States. Many youth believe that their legal status precludes them from going to college, which in fact is untrue. According to the College Board, there are no federal or state laws that prohibit the admission of undocumented immigrants to U.S. colleges and universities.[3] Yet, despite the actual absence of laws, the perception alone is often enough to prompt undocumented students to foreclose on a college-going identity. Certainly, these youth also face significant financial barriers to college enrollment (particularly because of their inability to access state and federal financial aid), but many of them do not even get to the point of considering their financial needs and options.

Because these identity processes are highly individual, and because they often operate subconsciously, practitioners need to provide opportunities for youth to engage in reflective discussions about them. Youth need open, safe spaces to consider the dimensions of their identities and to explore how these dimensions can be consistent with college and why they might not initially seem that way. Many youth do not have these opportunities in their daily lives, especially when it comes to discussing identity dimensions that are very central to beliefs about who they are and that are challenging for adults to discuss. For example, race and ethnicity are important elements of identity in the college-going process, but they are often not discussed, in part because many people feel uncomfortable discussing race, especially when talking with others from different racial and ethnic backgrounds. Or, as we have seen more often, some practitioners decide not to consider the influence of race (or issues of difference of any kind) instead taking a "color-blind" approach to their work. Both scenarios potentially miss out on critical parts of young people's college-going identities.

Because each person's identity is individual, each will identify more strongly with some groups than others. When considering whether they "belong" in college in general or specific colleges in particular, young people may ask a variety of questions, sometimes subconsciously and rarely out loud. Are there women in engineering programs? Will this young person be the only one from the inner city or the rural Midwest? Are there other Muslim students at this college? Each of these questions can influence whether and where young people envision themselves and, as a result, whether they seek out the supports to make that vision possible.

In addition to providing opportunities for dialogue, practitioners should also create opportunities to show youth that people who share their racial, ethnic, socioeconomic, and other characteristics can and do succeed in college. This often requires only slight modifications to existing practices. For example, many programs and youth workers engage "motivational speakers" who have followed successful postsecondary paths. This can be a powerful strategy, but in order for it to be most effective, the speakers need to share dimensions of identity with the young people, especially those dimensions that youth see as most central. For example, recruiting a Southeast Asian college student to discuss her path to college may do very little for the Southeast Asian adolescent who thinks that being in foster care is what makes her unlikely to go to college. Making a good match between youth and speakers requires a solid understanding of the various dimensions of adolescents' identities.

In addition to these approaches, which specifically discuss the connection between identity and college-going, helping youth to develop positive and robust racial and ethnic identities is an important strategy that confers a range of benefits for young people, which could include college-going. Research shows that when youth develop and maintain confidence in their abilities and positive attitudes about their cultural and racial backgrounds, they are more likely to have high academic achievement, positive future orientations, a strong self-concept, psychological well-being, and the ability to cope with and respond to discrimination. Building on this research, many youth development programs focus on helping youth build strong and positive cultural identities as a means to reduce risky behaviors and promote academic engagement achievement. In a similar way, college preparation programs could apply similar strategies to help youth affirm aspects of their identity and integrate this into their future planning. The American Youth Policy Forum (AYPF) has highlighted several interesting examples of such practices that are specifically designed for Native American youth. The programs featured in AYPF's report describe a range of native-oriented activities, such as raising young people's awareness of their cultural identity, connecting youth to tribal leaders and elders, and elevating youth interest in becoming leaders in their communities. These kinds of activities enable youth to develop positive orientations and associations with their cultures while also making good academic and social choices that will open a path to postsecondary success.

Dealing with Identity Conflicts

Because all people have multiple dimensions to their identities, youth may see some dimensions of their identities as consistent with college-going and others as inconsistent, and this inconsistency can cause them to struggle to form and maintain a solid college-going identity. This can happen for many reasons. For instance, first-generation college-bound students who see themselves as high achievers and devoted family members may experience guilt or discomfort when opportunities for social mobility conflict with family expectations or set them apart from the experiences of family members. Researcher Howard London has pointed out that first-generation students can feel discomfort with an experience he termed "breaking away."[4] This issue can affect both whether youth pursue college and where, because some youth are reluctant to move beyond the family identities they hold.

A similar conflict is sometimes experienced by youth from rural communities, where ties to family members and family businesses and farms tend to be strong. In fact, research shows that adolescents from rural communities are more likely to experience such identity conflicts than are adolescents from other communities, and that those who do experience these conflicts tend to have lower educational aspirations and to be less likely to enroll in college after high school, as well as to have more negative psychological outcomes. According to researcher Joel Hektner, rural students often fear that "moving up implies moving out," prompting some youth to lower their aspirations in order to remain in their community.[5]

Whether or not these kinds of identity conflicts are experienced based on first-generation status, home community (as in the rural example), race, ethnicity, or other factors, they can influence the success (or lack thereof) of efforts to engage youth in forming college-going identities. One of the important roles of practitioners is to help youth think about and validate all of the dimensions of their identities and to find ways to see them as mutually reinforcing college-going. Education expert Jeannie Oakes describes helping youth develop a "multicultural college-going identity." She points out that adults should create contexts and cultures that do not "force students to choose between the culture, language, and values of their community and the majority culture and values that are broadly, if unnecessarily, associated with high academic achievement," so that youth don't have to feel that they are sacrificing certain dimensions of their identities or connections to important people in their lives in order to go to college.[6] Oakes suggests that one of the ways to help youth shape a multicultural college-going identity is to create programs and environments where college-going is expected and seen as the norm for *all* youth, especially those for whom this is not traditionally the case.

Another way that practitioners can help youth integrate college-going with other aspects of their identities is to help them consider how a college degree can actually support the communities with which they identify. This is a shift from what we often see in practice, when adults encourage young people to distance themselves from their communities and go to college to "get out of the ghetto" or "move out of the 'hood." These practitioners are usually trying to convey that college is a "way out" of a community with few resources or a means of reaping the economic benefits afforded by social mobility and educational attainment. However, this framing can potentially reinforce or even create a dichotomy between going to college and being a member of the community, and can put youth in the position of having to choose one or the other.

We believe, instead, that adults should help youth link salient aspects of their identities and communities with college-going. One way to do this is to invite youth to identify aspects of their own communities that they would like to see changed or improved and then examine what roles those youth could play in being a part of that change and how going to college is one step along that path.

TRYING ON THE ROLE OF COLLEGE-GOER

Unlike some parts of one's identity that stay relatively constant, such as race or immigration, some identity dimensions can change over time in response to life changes, new experiences, or even changes in the social environment. These aspects are typically referred to as *role identities* and reflect the positions and responsibilities that people play in their lives. Role theory suggests that adopting a particular role identity comes from having opportunities to enact that role or to engage in activities that people in similar roles do. Without these experiential opportunities, the role is less likely to become part of identity. For example, a future teacher may begin to develop his teacher identity during a preservice practicum experience when given the opportunity to be responsible for an entire class and multiple lesson plans. Over time, when he begins to develop confidence managing a classroom, earning the respect of kids, or seeing a lesson plan come to life, this role becomes further integrated into his larger identity. Similarly, role theory suggests that youth can solidify college-going identities more effectively by trying on the role of college-goer rather than simply by thinking about college or even visiting a campus.

The fact that role identities can and do change means that when adults provide youth with new, college-related experiences, they provide opportunities for youth to develop or reinforce the role of college-goer. Like the preservice teacher, youth are more likely to adopt the role of college-goer when they have opportunities to engage in the behaviors and activities that college students do. To be sure, most youth do not experience this until they begin college; for many, their primary experience with colleges comes in the form of campus tours and visits. However, there are some opportunities to help youth engage in the college-going experience and therefore to develop the college-goer role during high school, which may solidify their commitment to applying to and enrolling in college. In a study of students in the College Now program, a precollege readiness and preparatory program in New York, Melinda Mechur Karp and her colleagues explored whether participation in a dual enrollment program—students enroll in college-level courses while still in high school—served as a mechanism to create a college student role identity. The study found that the experiences in the course—such as sitting in the class and meeting with the professor—shaped students' college student role identity.[7] Interestingly, the act of enrolling in the course had no effect on its own. It was the students' experiences of college that gave them opportunities to practice and learn new skills and behaviors that introduced and reinforced the new identity.

Although very little research has examined the specific process of role identity development in relation to college access, we believe that this is an important area for exploration. While not all students will have the opportunity to participate in dual enrollment courses, there are many ways to help students actively explore the college student role. For example, many college preparatory programs include residential experiences and summer college coursework. Like many college access efforts, however, these opportunities are most often available to students for whom the college-goer role is already a part of their identity. These students are easy to identify: they sign up for enrichment programs, they come to school and participate regularly, and they are good self-advocates. But to make a real difference in reducing gaps in access to higher education, opportunities such as dual enrollment courses and residential programs need to make concerted efforts to recruit students who aren't already approaching adults to find new opportunities.

OPPORTUNITIES FOR PRACTICE

Helping youth make connections between the aspects of their identities that are most meaningful to them and college-going goals is a critical yet often-missed step. Educators and youth practitioners at all levels should—and can—attend to the foundational experience of identity development and incorporate support for identity development into practices and policies. This does not mean that practitioners should end current efforts that target aspiration setting and use mentors to show the range of people who succeed college. However, these kinds of strategies are more likely to be effective when practitioners first set the context through relationships, conversations, and experiences that allow young people to explore their identities, examine how those identities can connect to college-going, and envision themselves as successful college students.

Accomplishing this means continuing to provide exploratory and affirming experiences for those youth whose college-going identities are already forming. It also means understanding why some youth do not envision themselves as college students and then utilizing differentiated approaches to support them, wherever they may be in the process of identity exploration.

The following are some specific strategies that can be embedded into existing practices or expanded to form new activities that support the development of a college-going identity.

- *Make the unconscious conscious.* One of the single most challenging parts of helping youth explore and understand their identities is the invisible nature of identity development. Some aspects of identity are so deeply embedded into thoughts and actions that youth are not conscious of them—including how they may be working either in concert or in competition with college-going. Activities that foster self-awareness and reflection are valuable to adolescents, but, unfortunately, they tend to be rare. Practitioners can help youth consider, explore, and integrate multiple dimensions of their identities through activities such as "Who am I?" writing exercises, collages, art projects, or group discussions. For youth who have had few opportunities to begin identity exploration, practitioners may choose to focus these activities

86

on identity in general. For youth who are further in their identity explorations, practitioners may help them think about how multiple dimensions of identity do or do not seem consistent with college-going and why. In either case, practitioners can encourage youth to integrate multiple dimensions of identity by asking them to describe themselves in different domains (school, home, community) and then helping them to see and resolve perceived conflicts. Doing so can help youth validate all of the dimensions of their identities and find ways to see them as mutually reinforcing.

- *Lead discussions about whether and why youth believe that "people like me" can and do go to college.* Young people need safe, comfortable spaces to talk about complex identity topics that are sometimes considered taboo or too charged, such as the roles of race and income in determining what is possible for them. Without putting these topics on the table, it is impossible for adults to help youth resolve conflicts and find the resources that are available to them. Practitioners can provide opportunities for youth to talk about what opportunities they perceive are open to them in relation to their race, class, or other dimensions of identity through structured discussion groups, online or social media–based peer discussions, literature and history lessons, and classroom projects. Such formal and informal conversations can provide practitioners a window into how youth make meaning of college options and exploratory activities and can allow them to develop practices or interventions to counteract negative group associations or low educational expectations. In our experience, adolescents are more than willing to engage in discussions about race, culture, ethnicity, sexual orientation, and various other dimensions of identity when give an open, safe space to do so.

- *Identify exploratory opportunities that allow youth to truly experience the role of college-goer.* Activities that simulate the college experience can go a long way toward making the idea of going to college less abstract and helping youth try on this new role. Few youth have such opportunities; colleges and universities host overnight events for prospective students but rarely include time for young people to "practice" being college students by meeting with an advisor or attending a meeting of a student affiliation group. Activities to help youth try on the role of college-goer could include dedicated programs such as dual enrollment or precollege summer programs, special events such as holding arts performances or debates on college campuses, and using college-like practices in high school activities, such as creating syllabi and course Web sites for high school courses.

- *Review program or school policies that might undermine identity exploration.* Behaviors such as skipping program activities, missing appointments and deadlines, and occasionally disengaging might seem to adults to reflect a lack of commitment to a college-going path. Yet these behaviors are part of healthy identity development. Because youth are trying on multiple identities and exploring whether and how they fit together, practitioners should strive to develop policies that balance high expectations with support for the normative processes of identity exploration. This includes examining eligibility and dismissal policies that turn away youth because of missed deadlines, conflicting demands on their time, or the occasional behavior problem. Alternatives include more flexible eligibility criteria and contingency policies that leave open doors to youth without lowering program or personal expectations or standards. In addition, educators and youth workers can engage youth in conversations about how to weigh multiple priorities and make decisions that support their college aspirations.

- *Include activities that allow youth to build strong ties to and feel proud of the groups with which they identify.* Young people are more likely to feel good about themselves and believe in their ability to construct positive futures when they feel good about the groups with which they associate themselves. For example, as we described above, youth who have strong and positive racial and ethnic identities demonstrate a range of social, emotional, and academic benefits, all of which lay the foundation for getting into and succeeding in college. Because many practitioners come from different racial, ethnic, cultural, and socioeconomic backgrounds than the youth with whom they work, one promising strategy is to partner with community agencies and organizations in which staff are more likely to share identity and characteristics with youth. Churches, youth programs, and neighborhood-based social service agencies have much to offer but are rarely recognized in academic or college preparation settings. For example, holding college fairs in community centers or churches, inviting leaders of local youth programs to college planning nights, inviting clergy and other community members to talk about their college-going paths, and partnering with neighborhood social service centers can demonstrate to youth the importance of college-going and the fact that college can be and often is consistent with the dimensions of their identity that they may not initially view that way. Other promising strategies include scheduling campus visits to minority-serving institutions (MSIs) and colleges with high percentages of students from certain religious, ethnic, or other identity groups and seeking support from campus-based youth affiliation groups (such as the lesbian, gay, bisexual, transgendered, questioning [LGBTQ] organizations) for upcoming college visits.

4

BELIEVING

Seeing College as Possible and Probable

Envisioning oneself as a college student is the first step on a successful path to higher education. But in order to take the next step, a young person needs to believe that he has the skills and abilities that will carry him down the whole road, even in the face of obstacles. In our work in schools and youth programs, we have often heard young people say, "I'm not 'college material'" even when they have come to believe that "people like me" succeed in college. It's no big surprise that these youth rarely end up pursuing higher education. As a result, when practitioners hear this phrase, they often go into active persuasion mode, saying things like, "Stop doubting yourself! Of course you're 'college material.' You just have to apply yourself." But in order to help youth believe that they can do it, practitioners need to take a step back and understand the root causes of youths' negative beliefs. Frequently, youths' beliefs about whether they are "college material" are shaped by how they feel about their abilities and their beliefs about what is possible for them in the present and in the future. Youth who hold positive beliefs about their abilities and their future options are more likely to feel empowered to take the necessary steps to realize their postsecondary dreams, whereas those who hold negative beliefs about themselves are more likely to foreclose on higher education.

By understanding these processes and the kinds of experiences that influence them, practitioners can help young people consider alternative views of themselves and their futures that make college-going more likely. As with so many of the processes described in this book, this is often about tweaking existing practices rather than adding more. Here we describe how encouraging youth to reflect on their experiences and to be more consciously aware of their self-appraisals can build on the foundation of the identity processes and set the stage for positive goal setting.

In this chapter, you will learn:

- How self-concept shapes college-going behaviors
- How young people's experiences, and more importantly, their interpretation of those experiences, influence their self-concepts
- Why aspirations and expectations are not the same thing
- How youth programs, college access initiatives, and schools can make small changes that make a big difference in students' self-concepts and future orientations

SELF-CONCEPTS FOR SUCCESS

At all ages and in all endeavors, people are more likely to set, pursue, and achieve their goals if they have positive self-concepts. Psychologists generally use the term *self-concept* to refer to the ways that people describe and evaluate themselves at a given moment in time. This is an umbrella term that encompasses a range of specific concepts and theories. We focus here on two concepts that are particularly relevant for college access and success: self-competence, which refers to how skilled people feel they are at certain things, and self-efficacy, which refers to how capable people feel in achieving goals.

Assessing Ability: Self-Competence

Self-competence describes the perceptions people have of their ability or, more simply, how good they think they are at something. According to psychologist Susan Harter, who has studied self-concept in children and youth of various ages, this form of self-evaluation is domain-specific and may apply to academic competence, peer competence, or athletic competence. (This makes self-competence distinct from the construct of global self-esteem, or how people evaluate their overall worth.) Although each of these domains may have some direct or indirect influence on college access and success, academic self-competence is most relevant.

Children and adolescents who perceive themselves as having high levels of academic competence are more engaged and self-motivated in school, perform better academically, exhibit higher expectations for success, and pursue more challenging academic goals. It's easy to see how these benefits could translate into youth seeing themselves as "college material" and how this view can then make them more likely to engage in the preparatory behaviors that are necessary for college. For example, if a student believes that he is "good in school," he will be more likely to see honors and advanced placement courses as possible and consistent with his identity and will also be more inclined to enroll in them when given the choice of courses, as well as to persist when the material in those courses becomes difficult. Similarly, students who have high academic self-competence and see themselves as "college material" will probably be more likely to prepare for standardized tests, complete admission and financial aid applications, and participate in enrichment programs. These youth are also more likely to have high expectations of getting into and succeeding in college. Conversely, if a young person has low academic self-competence, due to either real or perceived lack of academic skills, this might make him question whether he has the internal resources to be successful in college and come to see himself as not being "college material." If he does not develop a future-oriented self and clear goals, then he may become academically disengaged and decline chances to participate in enrichment programs and other opportunities.

Getting to Goals: Self-Efficacy

Just as young people need to believe that they have the skills to succeed, they also need to believe that they have the ability to achieve the goals that they set. Psychologist Albert Bandura introduced the term *self-efficacy* to refer to this belief. Like self-competence, self-efficacy and its associated outcomes are domain specific. For example, while a teacher might possess positive self-efficacy beliefs about her teaching skills, she may not hold positive self-efficacy beliefs about her technology skills. As a result, she would be very likely to volunteer to design and teach a new course but less likely to volunteer to utilize the newest form of technology to teach that course. Adolescents' self-efficacy beliefs determine whether they think college is possible, the degree to which they feel able to succeed in getting into and through college, and, ultimately, the kinds of goals they set and actions they take.

Four primary factors influence self-efficacy: mastery of experience (successfully engaging in activities related to the domain), vicarious learning (seeing others doing activities related to the domain), social persuasion (hearing others reinforce one's own ability to be successful), and affective states (emotional states, such as happiness and clear-headedness, which allow a person to judge oneself accurately). These factors can be demonstrated through a recent experience when a friend prompted one of us to consider running the Boston Marathon:

- *Mastery of experience*: I have run a few other road races and completed them successfully
- *Vicarious learning*: I have watched others run the Boston Marathon and can see myself in their shoes
- *Social persuasion*: Friends have told me that they believe I can run the marathon
- *Affective state*: I am in a positive state of mind and believe I am in a good position to assess my running ability

Just as these four factors influence self-efficacy for running and therefore the likelihood of running the marathon, they influence self-efficacy for college-going and, in turn, a college-going identity and the likelihood of applying and enrolling.

A Cycle of Success

Self-competence and self-efficacy are part of a cyclical process that shapes college-going identity and behaviors. Self-competence and self-efficacy shape whether youth pursue certain experiences and activities, and the results of these experiences provide feedback through which youth continually reassess their self-appraisals. For example, a young person who believes that she is good at math is likely to pursue advanced coursework in math, explore math-related college and career options, and take the SAT II math subject test. If she receives a high score on the test and high end-of-year marks in her math course, this will likely reinforce her beliefs about her ability and her career choices. However, if she begins to consistently receive low scores, she may reevaluate.

Practitioners can support a positive cyclical process by providing opportunities for youth to form positive concepts that are grounded in experience and supported by feedback. This means providing opportunities for them to build new skills and also helping them interpret those experiences and the feedback they receive in them. Both components are crucial; one without the other is not sufficient. Vague or unsupported statements such as "You're great" and "You can do anything you set your mind to" are not grounded in experience, and youth are therefore less likely to be convinced by them and internalize them. Yet, when youth participate in skill-building opportunities but are left to interpret them on their own, they may not develop the positive self-concepts that staff and mentors intend, especially when those opportunities are challenging. This was the case for Barbara, whose participation in a summer program made her question whether or not she really was "college material."

As a high-achieving high school junior, Barbara was selected to participate in a summer program at a small, academically rigorous women's college that was designed for exemplary young women with an interest in science and engineering. As she began

this prestigious four-week residential program, Barbara felt fortunate to have been given a scholarship. She was excited about learning new material that wasn't covered in her high school, which had been labeled "underperforming," and about getting a sense of what college life would be like, especially since she knew few people who had gone to college and had seen many of her friends drop out of high school.

However, after only a week of classes, she struggled with the work and began to question whether she could keep up with the other women in the program. Because the faculty members were so nice and supportive, she sought their counsel and asked questions, and she stayed up late into the night working on the assignments, which ultimately helped her to successfully complete the program. But she continued to find the academic work extremely difficult and often found herself wondering why the other young women did not appear to struggle as much as she did. By the end of the program, she concluded that she lacked the academic ability to do the work at a college like this one and returned home with a changed view of her academic competence. Although she remained committed to her goal of graduating from college, she now questioned whether she would be successful at a prestigious college. When she returned to her high school the following fall, she found herself reevaluating the list of possible colleges to which she might apply. When questioned about this by her parents, she looked down and quietly replied, "I realized those schools aren't right for me."

❖   ❖   ❖

Barbara never had the opportunity to discuss the concerns about her competence with anyone. Having such an opportunity might have allowed her to reflect on why she felt this way, whether it was justified, and what she could have done to change it. A developmentally aware teacher or counselor might have recognized the detrimental impact of the program on her self-competence and helped her to reconsider her negative feelings about herself. For example, those practitioners could have helped her understand the difference between academic ability and academic preparation and helped her find the additional academic supports she needed to feel prepared to succeed at a prestigious college. They might also have helped her find other opportunities for mastery that would boost her self-competence and counteract the negative effects of the summer program.

To be clear, we are not suggesting that all students have the capability to succeed at the most prestigious universities. But for youth like Barbara, who showed enough promise to receive a scholarship to a competitive program but whose confidence began to waver, these kinds of conversations can help them find the internal resources to seek out the kinds of supports they need to achieve their potential.

VISIONS OF THE FUTURE

Self-concept and self-efficacy are based largely in people's view of themselves in the present, but they shape how people see themselves in the future. People have many ways of thinking about themselves in the future. These include visions of themselves that they aspire to, believe are possible, hope for, and fear. Each of these visions of oneself in the future can play an important role in how they develop future orientations that include college.

Aspirations Versus Expectations

Postsecondary aspirations and expectations influence college-going from early on, even for young children who will not begin actually planning for college for many years. Research has shown that aspirations and expectations are related but distinct concepts. *Aspirations* refer to hopes and dreams, or what one hopes will happen; *expectations* refer to beliefs about the future, or what one believes is likely to happen. Separating these terms provides insight into a potential discrepancy that warrants attention and support from adults. There are many young people who may aspire to go to college but, for a variety of reasons, some of which are deeply rooted in dimensions of their identity, they do not expect to go. Remember the ninth-graders in chapter 1 who raised their hands because they aspired to go to college? Chances are that if that question had been followed by another one about the students' expectations to go to college, a few hands would have been lowered, and this may have explained why some of these students didn't end up attending college. There has been little research on how often this discrepancy occurs; however, research done on children's career aspirations has revealed a similar gap.[1] Researchers asked children what they wanted to be when they grew up and followed up later with questions about what they expected they would become. Indeed, the children provided different answers. One of the lessons from this study is that the role of supportive adults is not simply to raise aspirations but to identify when youth experience a discrepancy, help them understand where the discrepancy comes from, and help them resolve it. Focusing solely on aspirations without aiming to reshape low expectations, as many college access efforts do, is insufficient.

Decision Making and Support Matching

One of the reasons that aspirations and expectations are so important is that they shape whether students are, in the words of some higher education researchers, predisposed to attend college. Donald Hossler and his colleagues describe predisposition as the first step in a three-step college choice decision-making process, which includes *predisposition* (developing postsecondary aspirations and college-going goals), *search* (identification of possible postsecondary opportunities), and *choice* (selection of appropriate college). The case of Kris, a student one of us worked with in an afterschool arts program, demonstrates how the predisposition stage serves as a precursor for the other two stages. As a high school senior, Kris wanted to find a college program that would allow her to pursue her passion for dance but also develop another skill set in case her performing career didn't work out. Knowing what she wanted but not sure how or where to find it, Kris reached out to former teachers and informal mentors who blended their artistic and academic interests. She talked with them about their educational and career paths and asked them to suggest schools that might offer a blend of arts and academics. Kris's predisposition to find a college with these offerings prompted her to enter the search phase and ultimately gave her a set of parameters for navigating the choice phase.

Research has shown that not all young people experience the predisposition stage in the same way, and, as a result, they need different kinds of support. Educational researcher Kassie Freeman, who has applied Hossler's model to the experiences of African American students, has been particularly interested in the question of why there has been a discrepancy between high aspirations and low college enrollment rates among African American students. She conducted conversations with students from both an inner-city public school and a private school and identified three types of African American youth in the predisposition stage:

- *Knowers* are youth whose plans to go to college have never been in question and for whom college is simply part of their identity fabric.
- *Seekers* are those youth who have at some recent point come to believe that college is an option for them and have begun to try on that identity.
- *Dreamers* are those who believe that college is not possible, but they continue to fantasize about it without any intention of taking any of the steps to get there.

Freeman's research points out that adults should consider what types of activities and programs are most useful to which groups. Connecting knowers to a nonprofit agency that helps youth fill out college applications will likely be beneficial, whereas connecting dreamers with this kind of support will likely be ineffective, because these youth first need activities designed to elicit why they foreclosed. Connecting all youth to the kinds of supports they need requires differentiating programs and services in order to meet each youth where she is on the continuum of predisposition. This is particularly important in order to reach the students who are seekers and dreamers, those who have not already embraced the role of college-goer.

Possible Selves

As Hossler's and Freeman's work acknowledge, aspirations, predispositions, and expectations drive how people behave in planning for and working toward their futures. The framework of *possible selves*, introduced by Hazel Markus and Paula Nurius, is helpful for understanding how these kinds of beliefs about oneself translate into motivation and, ultimately, action. Possible selves are representations that people hold about themselves in the future. They can include the selves that people hope to become, expect to become, and fear becoming. Examples consist of everything from the happy self to the athletic self to the college-going self, and from the unsatisfied self to the overweight self to the drifter self. Each possible self can be powerful enough on its own to motivate action. For example, a strong hoped-for self as a doctor can spur a young person to work hard in biology class and to find an internship at a hospital, and a strong feared self as an unemployed person can spur a student to raise his failing grades. But sometimes one possible self is not enough on its own. Sometimes the hoped-for self as college-goer is not enough to motivate a student to study or complete a college application because other competing desires and demands (like hanging out with friends or working extra shifts at a part-time job) are too strong. In this case, a hoped-for self is more likely to motivate action if it is reinforced by a feared self.

This is illustrated in the case of Muhammad, a young man who is portrayed in *The College Track: America's Sorting Machine*. In this Films for the Humanities and Sciences video series, Muhammad describes his dream of going to college, which can be thought of as a hoped-for self as college-goer.[2] But he also has a strong feared self, as he describes when he explains how his father's work demands provide him a window into a world he doesn't want for himself: "For the working life for my father, I don't like it because he works twenty-four seven. He works like a robot, a horse, or whatever. He [works] nonstop. I can't work like that. It's not about laziness, it's about just wanting to have a better opportunity in life." Muhammad's feared self as a laborer reinforced his hoped-for self and therefore made it even more likely he would take the steps necessary to get to college.

It is important to point out that this counterbalancing of hoped-for and feared selves can work in the opposite direction as well. Muhammad's feared self was helpful because he could see an alternative. But if he had not seen an alternative—that is, did not have a hoped-for self as a college-goer—his feared self would not necessarily have helped motivate him and might, in fact, have resulted in feelings of frustration or distress. It is therefore important to help young people develop and utilize both kinds of possible selves so that when one is insufficient or potentially detrimental, they can use the other as well.

Research by Daphna Oyserman has found that possible selves affect academic and college-going behaviors as well as a wide range of other academic and social outcomes. Based on this research, Oyserman has developed school-based interventions designed to help youth reach their hoped-for selves and avoid their feared selves. In many of her interventions, Oyserman and her colleagues ask youth to create "Possible Me Trees" that engage participants in developing visual representations of their goals and dreams and that utilize the hoped-for self.[3] This type of activity also asks youth to articulate their fears about these future-oriented goals to help them develop strategies for moving beyond those fears and reducing the likelihood of negative outcomes. Through helping youth make concrete both hoped-for and feared selves, these activities maximize the likelihood that youth will turn their beliefs about themselves and their futures into action even when one type of future self feels far off or unimportant.

UNDERSTANDING THE SELF IN A SOCIAL CONTEXT

Although people's beliefs about themselves and their future possibilities are internal processes, they are strongly influenced by social contexts and experiences and the meaning that people make of them. In particular, people's own perceptions of themselves are influenced by how other people see them. Early theorists referred to this as the *looking-glass self*, because people use feedback from others like a mirror, forming their self-concepts through what they hear and see much like how they come to understand their physical appearance by looking in the mirror. Practitioners can play a role in this process. Sometimes they serve as the mirrors, sending messages to young people about their traits and strengths. Other times, friends and acquaintances serve as mirrors, but practitioners can step in to help young people reinterpret negative feedback. And at still other times, practitioners are not and cannot be involved. Either way, being aware of how social influences affect self-concept is helpful for understanding why young people see themselves the way they do, how those perceptions may be helpful or detrimental, and where opportunities exist to support healthy and positive self-concepts that support college-going. A comprehensive list of social influences on identity is beyond the scope of this chapter, but we highlight a few examples here that are particularly relevant for first-generation college students.

A large body of research shows that parents influence their children's and adolescents' aspirations, expectations, and views of themselves. This occurs, in part, through the messages that parents send about their own beliefs in their children's abilities and, in part, through the messages they send about how much they value education, expect children to do well, and believe that college is possible and desirable. This is one of the many reasons that it is so important to make families partners in college access, not only to help families see the importance of college but to encourage them to view college as possible and see the routes to get there. Many families do not believe that college is possible due to financial and other reasons, and they may foreclose early, just as adolescents do. Reaching families as early as elementary school and continuing to reach out to them during middle school and high school, when planning becomes so important, can help them develop and convey high expectations for their children's postsecondary paths.

The culture of schools, extracurricular programs, and communities also shape young people's views of themselves and their futures. Beyond the influence of individual counselors or administrators, young people are influenced by the social norms and organizational beliefs in the settings where they spend their time. This is why many schools have adopted approaches to promoting a college-going culture and why many youth development programs make an explicit point about conveying high postsecondary expectations for all participating youth. When coupled with strong academic preparation and support, these expectations and norms can affect youths' views of themselves in the present and the future.

Clearly, there are many positive ways that social contexts and relationships support healthy self-appraisals and self-aspirations. However, on the negative side, people's perceptions of themselves and what is possible for them can also be influenced by stereotypes and/or more overt forms of discrimination. Social psychologist Claude Steele discovered a phenomenon that he refers to as *stereotype threat*, which explains why people who are members of frequently stereotyped groups (such as racial, gender, and religious groups) may be more likely to actually perform in ways that are consistent with that stereotype. Steele's research suggests that stereotypes subconsciously and negatively affect individuals' beliefs about what they can do.[4] This is particularly true in situations when the person's minority status is highlighted. For example, in laboratory studies Steele has found that women perform more poorly on math tests when they are in a room full of men. This is especially true when the experimenter tells the women ahead of time that men usually outperform women on the test. Surprisingly, it also happens even without that prompting. In other words, the stereotype occurs subconsciously. In the real world, this makes stereotypes even more insidious and difficult to counteract unless they are made explicit and deconstructed. Studies have suggested that stereotype threat operates for members of all kinds of stereotyped groups, including African American and Latino students, and even for white students when contrasted with Asian American students.

To our knowledge, stereotype threat has not yet been studied in relation to college access. But it is certainly plausible that some of the youth who are from underrepresented groups and who are not achieving their full postsecondary potential are acting (perhaps subconsciously) in accordance with a belief that "people like me are not capable of succeeding in college." For practitioners, becoming mindful about these invisible processes is critical because they shape all of the other influential components of identity that we have discussed. Being mindful includes becoming aware of personal biases and acceptance of stereotypes. Practitioners should ask themselves questions such as, "Do we subconsciously set up different expectations for youth from different backgrounds?" and "Do our conversations with boys and girls about career interests follow a similar pattern?" In addition to engaging in this kind of reflective practice, it may also help to encourage youth to reflect on their own strengths in the domain in which they might feel threatened, particularly encouraging them to affirm the skills, values, and assets that can help them ward off threatened feelings.

Practitioners from different disciplines also have some unique opportunities to help combat stereotype threat. Teachers can help students reflect on their academic performance and convey messages that performance is due to effort rather than innate ability, which some students may subconsciously associate with group identity. College program staff can highlight the success stories of people from traditionally underrepresented groups (which tend to also be stereotyped) through mentoring partnerships, lectures and speeches, or even books and movies.

OPPORTUNITIES FOR PRACTICE

In order to help youth enact the college-going identities we described in chapter 3, practitioners need to provide opportunities for youth to develop realistic, positive views of themselves as capable individuals who can and will succeed in college—to help them move beyond envisioning themselves in college to believing that they can be successful. With this foundation, youth are then more likely to join in programs and other college access activities and, of course, to get more out of them. Many practitioners are well-positioned to do this work, but practitioners who work outside the traditional domains of college access programs tend to have much experience and many lessons to offer in providing opportunities for youth to develop skills and the self-concepts that come from those skills. The strategies we present here can be used in collaborations among different kinds of practitioners or by individuals, and they can also be applied to policies and programmatic structures:

- *Create opportunities for youth to assess their assets.* Very few of us are good at acknowledging our strengths. Outside of a job interview, when was the last time you thought about what you are good at? Youth are particularly notorious for not being aware of their strengths, fearing that they do not have any strengths, or perhaps feeling that their strengths are unimportant. It is therefore important to find ways to enable young people to build on their assets rather than to dwell on what they see as their deficiencies. This can serve as a useful foundation for shaping future goals and behaviors. This strength-based approach can be applied to learning, aspiration, and goal setting. One way to accomplish this is through the use of strengths-based asset mapping, in which young people are encouraged to identify their assets, specifically in areas that inform their self-concept. For example, adolescents can create actual maps or engage in writing assignments that invite them to respond to such questions as "What makes you feel successful?" or "What have you done to support your own success?" In this example, adolescents might map critical or influential relationships that make them feel good or competent.
- *Provide opportunities for youth to build skills and then reflect on those skills.* Promoting youths' self-concepts is about

helping them form realistic positive views of themselves, not about raising their self-competence in an empty or isolated way. To feel a deep sense of self-competence and to believe that they can achieve their goals, youth must have experiences of success on which to draw. This requires that youth programs, schools, and other contexts provide ample opportunities for young people to develop skills in a range of areas and interests, which can include academics, arts, sports, technology, cooking, and many other areas. Youth development programs can serve as a model for how to do this work. Many afterschool and enrichment programs are specifically designed to provide youth with opportunities to develop their skills and to then reflect on those experiences in ways that help them develop self-efficacy and strong self-concepts and think about the future.

- *Assist youth in transferring self-efficacy from one domain to another.* Research on skill theory suggests that the skills that individuals develop in particular domains do not necessarily lead to the development of other skills. (Just because a young woman excels on the basketball court does not mean she will have the same success in the classroom, and vice versa.) However, the sense of confidence and competence that youth derive from their success in one area can be transferred to new tasks, giving them the persistence to develop the skills needed to succeed. (The athlete can learn that her hard work and dedication on the court have allowed her to succeed in basketball and take from this the belief that she is a hard worker who has the ability to succeed in school when she applies the same effort.) Adults play an important role in helping youth draw those connections. Doing so may prompt youth to take healthy risks, move beyond their comfort zone, or challenge themselves in an unfamiliar arena.

- *Set the stage for balanced goal setting.* There are many creative ways to help youth set possible, hoped-for, and feared goals. For example, middle school students might create "Possible Me Trees" in which they develop visual representations of their goals and dreams and that utilize the hoped-for self. This type of activity also asks youth to articulate their fears about the future to help them develop strategies for moving beyond those fears and reducing the likelihood of the negative outcomes. Positive visualization techniques from clinical psychology, especially the field of cognitive behavioral therapy, can be useful here. Facilitated opportunities that bring into awareness what youth want to avoid will help them identify strategies for keeping them at bay and working in pursuit of their hoped-for goals.
- *Utilize tools that promote self-appraisal.* Interest inventories, reflective exercises, and case studies provide youth with information from which they make sense of who they are and open doors to engage in conversations about how youth make meaning of their strengths and talents, or their lack thereof. These types of self-assessments also provide a window for practitioners to identify where misinformation or incorrect perceptions of ability may exist and intervene accordingly. For example, there is a growing trend to use college placement tests with high school students as a means to identify gaps in skills and knowledge necessary for college readiness. This type of early assessment can have enormous benefit when

coupled with reflective conversations and academic support to build the additional skills necessary to be ready
for college at a later point in the educational pathway.
However, when the results of these assessments, and
others like them, such as the PSAT, are presented to
youth without support for how to interpret and build
on them, such initiatives run the risk that youth will
misinterpret the results as evidence that they are not
really "college material."

- *Be mindful of approaches that undermine the development of
  self-efficacy.* Whereas persuasion and encouragement
  play a key role in increasing self-efficacy, especially if the
  source of the verbal persuasion is credible and trustwor-
  thy, there are subtle ways that adults can undermine adolescents' self-efficacy. Not assigning challenging tasks,
  constantly offering unsolicited help, and doing things
  for youth rather than allowing them to demonstrate and
  experience mastery of a skill will all subtly undermine
  their ability to feel effective at a given task or set of tasks.

5

AIMING

Setting Goals That Set Up Success

*M*otivation is a word that we hear a lot among practitioners. We hear it in positive statements like, "Our program motivates young people to go to college," and we also hear it in negative statements like, "If my students were more motivated, I could help them more." But what exactly *is* motivation, and what does it mean for a young person to be motivated for college or for a program to promote motivation?

Many people believe that motivation is simple and clearcut: youth who say they want to enroll in and graduate from college are motivated, whereas those who don't have these goals are unmotivated. But contrary to popular belief, motivation is not something that people either have or don't have; motivation cannot be measured in terms of "how much." Motivation is something that must be understood qualitatively and descriptively. Motivation is a cyclical process involving the kinds of goals people set, the reasons they set them, and the actions they take to achieve them. The question, then, is not whether people are motivated, but what they are motivated for and why. Consider the case of these two hypothetical adolescents:

Adrian and Jesse sit side by side, waiting for their eleventh-grade math teacher, Ms. James, to return the results of their SAT practice tests. Adrian gets good grades in his classes, has been studying regularly for the SAT, and shadows a veterinarian after school, all while working at a local grocery store to help support his family. When asked about his post–high school plans, Adrian says, "I want to find a college with good science programs, because I want to be either a vet or a neuroscience researcher. I'm not sure which one. I love taking care of animals, but I saw a TV show about advances in neuroscience, and I think it would be really cool and exciting to discover something new about the brain. Whichever one I pick will probably be great, because science is really interesting and makes me feel really inspired."

In contrast, Jesse puts in the bare minimum effort in his classes and spends most of his free time hanging out at a local park with his friends. He doesn't plan to apply to college and took the practice test only because it was required during class. When Ms. James caught him after class one day and asked about his plans, Jesse responded by saying, "I dunno. My friend's dad is opening a body shop, and he might have a job for me. I've never really been into cars, but my friend says it pays well, and my dad would be happy because then I'd have a real skill, which he's says I've never had." Hearing this, Ms. James looked Jesse in the eye and said, "Being a mechanic is a great career, Jesse—both intellectually and physically challenging. But is that what you really want to do?" Jesse shrugged and said, "I dunno. I don't really care."

As she flips through the practice tests before handing them back, Ms. James reflects on this conversation and wonders, "Why isn't Jesse motivated by anything? Why isn't he more like Adrian, who is very motivated?"

❖ ❖ ❖

Ms. James assumed that motivation is something that young people have or don't have, and in so doing she missed an important opportunity to understand Jesse and his future path. Instead of wondering, "Why isn't he motivated?" she should have been asking, "What is he motivated for, and why doesn't it line up with the things I would hope him to be motivated for— like a career that he finds interesting?" What Ms. James didn't see is that Jesse was motivated by a different set of goals than Adrian. These may have included hanging out with friends and living in the neighborhood where his whole extended family has lived for decades. They may have included the desire to make his father proud. Or they may have included the desire to avoid looking like a failure if he applied and didn't get into college. Each of these goals has very different meanings and different implications for Jesse's future. Similarly, the factors affecting Jesse's goals—including his values, his beliefs about himself, and his interpretations of the factors that cause success and failure—have important implications.

We describe here the nature and development of goals and the kinds of practices that can help young people develop the motivational processes that will help them aspire to, enroll in, and succeed in college, going beyond *whether* adolescents aspire to college to *why* they do or do not, and how this influences their behaviors in both preparing for college and persisting once there. Understanding this process can help practitioners more effectively reach all youth, especially those who are not knock-ing down adults' office doors asking for help, those whom practitioners may label with the misnomer "unmotivated."

In this chapter, you will learn:

- Why goals are an important part of the college-going process and how they shape behaviors both before and during college
- Why financial and other external rewards are not enough to ensure college success
- Why going to college to please others is not sufficient
- How adults' everyday interactions with young people shape college-going goals and outcomes

MAKING MEANING AND MAKING PROGRESS

Much of what is known about motivation—including the cen-tral role of goals and the reasons that people pursue them—is based on the work of psychologist Albert Bandura, whose so-cial cognitive theory of motivation has informed hundreds of research studies and the development of more nuanced theo-ries of everything from peer relationships to career planning. This theory points out that motivation is an active process that is about the meaning that people make of their experiences, not a passive state that can be imparted to them by others.

As Bandura has explained, goals play a large role in this ac-tive process because they shape behaviors, which affect out-comes, which then shape the meaning that people make of the whole process and therefore how they set other goals in the future. For example, if I set a goal of running a marathon, I will engage in behaviors that help me train, which may include regular practice runs that get longer over time, daily stretching, and eating in ways that help maintain a healthy weight. My goal (like all goals) is shaped largely by how I feel about myself, my ability, and my likelihood of success. This is one of the reasons that self-efficacy, which we described in detail in chapter 4, is so important: I am more likely to set the marathon-running goal if I believe that I am strong enough and disciplined enough to do it and that I am likely to make it the whole 26.2 miles (after training, of course). This whole chain of events is influenced by social context, including my environment and the people within it. I am more likely to feel capable of training for and completing the marathon if I have access to a safe, weather-appropriate place to train and if I feel that my family and friends will provide the moral and instrumental support I need, such as encouraging me when I hit the exhausting midpoint of the training schedule and taking care of my children on the day of the big event. All of these things operate in an ongoing cycle: the experience of running the marathon, including whether I finish and how much I enjoy it, will either reinforce or change my beliefs about my ability, which will then influence whether I set a goal to run another marathon, and so on.

Bandura's theory is highly useful in understanding goal setting and motivation for future planning. In fact, Robert Lent, Steven Brown, and Gail Hackett adapted it as social cognitive career theory. In this theory, career interests and options, along with self-efficacy, predict career goals, which, in turn, influence actions and behaviors, which shape the kind of feedback loop described above. Again, social influences and environment play an important part in all stages of this process. A young person who has an interest in the theater might be inclined to take a class in lighting design at a community arts center, where he excels and receives praise for his effort and skill from his teacher and peers. The positive outcome of this experience then reinforces his career interest, which spurs him to sign up for a summer arts program and investigate colleges with courses in technical theater. On the contrary, if the outcome of his experience is negative, chances are his efficacy in this area would go down, thereby affecting future goals.

The fact that a supportive environment can help people set more challenging goals and feel more capable of attaining those goals means that educators and youth workers have important roles to play. Just as my family members play a role in whether I run the marathon, practitioners have roles to play in helping youth set and achieve college-going goals. This is the social part of social cognitive theory.

But the cognitive part, which refers to the meaning that the individual makes of her experiences, is equally important. Whether the individual is my marathon-striving self or a college-bound high school student, that individual has to be an active agent in constructing the goals, seeing the supports from the environment, and interpreting her experiences and abilities and how they influence the likelihood of success. Motivation ultimately has to come from within, but it is affected by other people and environmental factors. Adults cannot impart motivation to young people, but they can do things to help them engage in a process that psychologists refer to as *adaptive motivation*: forming the beliefs, goals, and behaviors that are conducive to success and well-being. This includes helping youth set the kinds of goals that will make them most likely not only to aspire to and enroll in college but also to persist and succeed once there.

GOALS THAT HELP AND GOALS THAT DON'T

The fact that goals play a large part in motivation may seem like common sense, and Albert Bandura was certainly not the first person to understand that goals are important. But social cognitive theory has spurred research about what kinds of goals are most effective for increasing the likelihood of success and how. This body of research tells us that the reasons youth pursue college matter, especially in determining whether youth persist when they encounter challenges. For example, it has informed research suggesting that focusing exclusively on the financial rewards that come with a college degree or on meeting the expectations and hopes of families, teachers, or other significant people can actually make young people less likely to succeed in the long term.

Why Extrinsic Rewards Alone Won't Result in College Success

Thinking back to the case we described at the beginning of this chapter, Adrian's and Jesse's future plans were focused on different kinds of outcomes and rewards. Adrian, who was excited about a career in science, was driven by intrinsic motivation. According to psychologists Edward Deci and Richard Ryan's self-determination theory, when *intrinsically motivated*, a person performs a task for its inherent interest or enjoyment. The task is its own reward. A high school student who is intrinsically motivated for college and career may be looking forward to the opportunity to conduct interesting science experiments, like Adrian, or to hone her writing so that she can become a journalist. In contrast, when *extrinsically motivated*, a person performs a task for the purpose of receiving external rewards. Those rewards can be tangible, such as money or prizes, or they can be intangible, such as high grades, prestige, or respect from others. We have seen many adolescents who are extrinsically motivated for college because they are driven by the promise of a higher income or by having the names of prestigious universities on their resumes.

Deci and Ryan have also described a third kind of motivation that falls between intrinsic and extrinsic motivation. This form of motivation, *internalized regulation*, occurs when people value and pursue activities that they do not find intrinsically interesting but that they believe will help them reach their ultimate goals. The key to this kind of motivation is that people internalize extrinsic rewards in ways that allow them to feel ownership of the goal and the reward. Aiming to score well on the SAT/ACT is a good example. This goal and the process of attaining it may not be inherently rewarding (at least for most people), but young people can value it as a means to attaining an intrinsic goal such as beginning the path to an interesting career.

Distinguishing among these different types of motivation is essential to understanding why some youth are more successful at reaching the goals they set for themselves than others. When driven by intrinsic motivation and internalized regulation, youth are more likely to choose challenging tasks, retain information, and perform well academically. This makes it more likely that they will aspire to college and develop the skills to get there. Even more importantly, intrinsic motivation and internalized regulation make adolescents more likely to persist and succeed once they get to college.

In contrast, when they are extrinsically motivated, people tend to perform equally well on rote learning tasks, but they demonstrate less conceptual learning and creativity and tend to avoid challenges. Extrinsic motivation is particularly problematic in the long run. One reason is that when people are extrinsically motivated, they depend on structures in the environment in the form of either rewards (which they pursue) or sanctions (which they intentionally avoid). When those structures are no longer available, the motivation disappears. A colleague of ours illustrated this with the example of his ever-mounting pile of speeding tickets. Although he has a tendency to drive over the speed limit, he complies with the law at certain spots along the highway where he knows that state troopers frequently set up speed traps. But as soon as he passes those spots, he speeds again. (Unfortunately for him and his insurance premium, he's not very good at predicting where the state troopers patrol outside of those known speed traps.) Because he is motivated only by the desire to avoid the extrinsic sanction (the speeding ticket), his behavior has not changed in a meaningful or permanent way. If instead he focused on and internalized the benefits of the speed limit (such as other drivers' safety), he would be more likely to stop speeding even in places where he is unlikely to encounter a speed trap. Because our colleague is a good person who genuinely cares about the welfare of others, simply having frequent reminders from friends, family, and authority figures would probably help him internalize the benefits of the speed limit and change his behavior in a more long-lasting way.

In the same way that the speeding tickets have not yet led our colleague to change his driving habits, extrinsic educational rewards do not, on their own, lead young people to establish long-term habits that support college planning, enrollment, and success. Schools and colleges tend to reward extrinsic motivation, especially in the short run, because youth who are focused on getting good grades and winning awards are seen as competent, hard working, and successful. But when those extrinsic rewards disappear, either in college, graduate school, or the workplace, people who are motivated solely by those things tend to become lost, feel confused, or stop engaging in the behaviors that originally made them successful.

Extrinsic rewards become less available during college and after, and as a result, we have seen this motivational slump occur many times with both college and graduate students. For example, the population of students who are most likely to attend competitive master's and doctoral programs are often those who were motivated by and received extrinsic rewards for their high academic performance. But when they begin their graduate training, we have heard many say, "What do you mean my grades don't matter in graduate school? What am I working for now, and how will I know if I'm successful?" Because they have to create and carry out independent projects that are not dictated by someone else, some of them become so daunted that they struggle to establish or finish these projects. In contrast, those graduate students who have received high grades and many accolades but also have an intrinsic passion for the work tend to thrive in graduate programs, where they have the freedom and responsibility to shape their own projects and careers.

Why Solely Aiming to Please Others Won't Result in College Success

In addition to focusing on the financial benefits of college, many youth are driven by a desire to please their families and other supporters. We have seen this be a particularly powerful reason for youth whose parents have not gone to college themselves but who have worked hard to help their children get to college. This desire to make family members proud can help youth envision a college-going future and begin to think of college as both possible and worthwhile. However, on its own, this kind of goal is not enough to ensure that youth will persist in the challenging processes of getting to college and graduating. The case of Jay, a first-generation college-bound student illustrates this.

Jay had planned to go to college for as long as he could remember. Ever since he was a little boy, his parents had been constantly telling him that an education is essential for a good life. They reminded him of this just as they reminded him of all they had sacrificed to emigrate to the United States from their home country of Cambodia. For most of their schooling, Jay and his brother hadn't approached studying and learning as things they wanted to do; these were things that they had to do. Jay's parents were very proud and clearly satisfied when Jay brought home good report cards and high marks on papers, and they talked often about how these grades would get him into a good college. But as he looked toward the future, Jay secretly wasn't sure he wanted to go to college, believing that it would just feel like a continuation of the strenuous routine and academic pressure he had been experiencing since he was a child. He didn't know what kind of career he wanted to develop for himself, and he worried that he would end up just going to college to satisfy his parents' expectations and not really get much out of it.

However, something changed for Jay when he was in tenth-grade English class: he developed a passion for writing. Although he had not previously enjoyed writing, his English teacher allowed students to select topics that were meaningful to them, and this engaged Jay in a way that he had never experienced before. In his first assignment, he wrote about his experience on the boat coming to America from Cambodia. Writing about something that was deeply important to him, and having the opportunity to connect his experience with others' when he read aloud his essay to the class, changed Jay's opinion about writing, and it gave him a new focus for his schoolwork and his future. Fueled by this new passion, Jay suddenly sought to learn everything he could about writing: he began to seek out feedback from his English teacher, even when it wasn't required; he became a voracious reader; and he applied to a summer young writers' conference. He also began looking at colleges with affiliated writers' workshops.

In eleventh grade, Jay was introduced to a freshman from the local college through a college awareness and preparation program. In his conversations with this "college advisor," Jay spoke at length about his interest in writing. Together they looked at colleges and courses that focused on writing. He was amazed by the range of courses in college that just focused on writing and was excited by the prospect of having more time to write and plenty of opportunities for feedback from faculty. With a newfound purpose for attending college, Jay enthusiastically worked with his school counselors and his advisor to prepare for the SATs and used part of his summer to begin essays for college applications.

Jay's story illustrates that going to college solely to please others isn't enough on its own, and that young people are more likely to succeed when they own the goal of college. Research, which is supported by our experience, suggests that if Jay had not developed his own reasons for going to college and had continued to be driven solely by his parents' desires, his motivation for college would have waned. This decrease in motivation can happen at many points in the college-going process. While aiming to please others is not the sole reason for its occurrence, it is a common one.

Youth who find themselves going through the motions of college planning without real ownership and intrinsic interest in the process are often the ones we see step off the path at key transition points. Psychologist Karen Arnold and her colleagues have shown that the summer between high school and college is one particularly vulnerable transition point for first-generation college students. These researchers have coined the term "summer flood" to describe the phenomenon of young people failing to enroll in higher education despite their plans to do so at the end of the senior year.[1] Among several of the reasons for this phenomenon that Arnold and her colleagues have found is the fact that focusing strictly on meeting others' expectations can cause college-bound youth to lose their way. They quote a young person who describes how aiming to please others can cause problems for youth not only during the summer transition, but even for youth who have made it past that point: "there's a difference between wanting to go to college and someone telling you they want you to go to college. Because when you go to college for reasons you don't know why, then you drop out. Because you don't know why you're there. You're going for someone else. It's like a promise you're keeping that's not yours. It's not your own promise."[2]

Achievement goal theory provides a helpful frame for understanding this phenomenon. Achievement goal theory, which is closely related to Deci and Ryan's theory about extrinsic and intrinsic motivation, adds a social focus that is particularly useful for understanding the processes that occur when young people pursue college in order to please their families, friends, or educators. According to achievement goal theory, *mastery goals* (sometimes called learning goals) are focused on improving knowledge and ability. *Performance goals* (sometimes called ego goals) are focused on the desire to demonstrate ability or to avoid looking incompetent to peers, parents, educators, bosses, and others. To return to the marathon example, running for the sake of increasing strength or developing a new skill would be considered mastery goals. Running to impress an athletic sibling or to avoid being the only one of my friends not to complete a marathon would be considered performance goals. Needless to say, I might run the marathon for all of those reasons. Although some people may be more inclined to set mastery or performance goals, they can set multiple kinds of goals at the same time. The kinds of goals they set may also change over time, even for the same activities. For example, Jay's plan to apply to college was initially driven by a performance goal (to please his parents) but shifted to a mastery goal (to pursue his interest in writing).

The likelihood of setting certain kinds of goals is shaped in part by relationships and experiences. For Jay, these relationships included those with his parents, his English teacher, and his college student advisor. They are also shaped by cultural values. For example, many studies find that performance goals are more common among youth from cultures that place a high value on collectivism, interdependence, and performing well in order to bring pride to the family (such as many Asian cultures) and among youth from immigrant families whose parents, like

Jay's, have often sacrificed a great deal in order to attain an education for their children. This is not to suggest that youth from these cultures are driven solely by these kinds of goals, but rather that these kinds of goals tend to be more present for or feel more central to youth from more collectivistic cultures.

Overall, research shows that mastery goals are associated with a wide range of positive outcomes similar to those associated with intrinsic motivation. Performance goals, like extrinsic motivation, tend to be associated with negative outcomes, including less persistence and lower psychological well-being. This is particularly true when people set performance goals out of fear of performing badly or looking incompetent. Researchers refer to these goals as *performance-avoidance goals*. We hear examples of performance-avoidance goals when young people say things like "I have to go to college because I'll let my parents down if I don't" and "My coach will think I'm dumb if I tell him I got a low score on the SAT."

Applying this to college access, we see that youth who plan for, enroll in, and engage in college for the sake of learning new skills and information (mastery goals) are more likely to succeed, perform well, and persist than those who are there solely to prove that they can do it, or to avoid the disappointment of their families, friends, or communities. The latter group of youth are less likely to internalize their commitment to higher education, which can lead them to question why they are there, become confused when confronted with decisions about their own futures, be less interested in the work, and even to get swept into the summer flood or drop out of college before graduating.

We've seen this phenomenon operate in many situations, across many cultures, and in many communities. These include communities with high percentages of first-generation college students, especially youth from immigrant families like Jay's, or from low-income families in which being the first to go to college and break out of poverty are very central goals not only for the youth but for their parents. These goals, and the needs that drive them, can play a very important role for many youth. But time and again, we have seen that when youth are focused *only* on these goals, they struggle emotionally and academically in college. In contrast, the youth we have seen who are *also* driven by strong mastery goals tend to thrive in college and beyond. We have seen this illustrated most clearly in young people who have initially gone to college to please others and left after having little success but then have gone on to re-enroll and succeed once they have found career interests that provided the intrinsic motivation to go back to college.

One of the reasons that a strong focus on performance goals can be detrimental is that these kinds of goals are insufficient to motivate youth when they subsequently encounter challenges, including poor performance and setbacks such as financial difficulties or juggling the demands of education, work, and family. These challenges are a common part of obtaining a college degree, not only during the application process but especially during the college years. And when youth encounter these challenges—as almost all of them do at some point—if they are motivated solely by a desire to avoid looking incompetent or to make their family and friends proud, they are less likely to tough it out through the challenges and more likely to give up.

When young people are mastery oriented and focused on learning, they tend to respond to poor performance in produc-

128

tive ways, often attributing their performance to lack of effort and resolving to work harder in the future. But when they are performance oriented and concerned with demonstrating ability, they tend to respond in what psychologist Carol Dweck calls a *learned helpless* way: they attribute their poor performance to lack of ability and, in order to protect their self-esteem, reduce their effort in the future. Again, these contradictory patterns can be seen in the cases of Adrian and Jesse.

When their math teacher, Ms. James, hands back the SAT practice tests, both Adrian and Jesse find out that they have scored below 1100. Adrian, who is disappointed by his performance, sighs and says, "I know I can do better than this. I was so busy the month before the test that I didn't have time to study as much as I should have. I guess I'll have to work harder next time." Jesse, however, chuckles as he tosses the paper in his bag and says under his breath, "I knew it. I'm not smart enough to go to college. Why even bother studying?"

When they received lower test scores than they would have hoped, Adrian attributed his performance to lack of effort and believed that he could do better if he worked harder in the future. Jesse, on the other hand, reacted with learned helplessness, attributing his failure to lack of ability, and gave up. From elementary school through college, learned helplessness leads people like Jesse to use less efficient strategies, perform more poorly on academic tasks, avoid challenges, and give up when confronted with poor performance. As a result, we would expect them to be less likely to go to college and less likely to graduate even if they do enroll.

The Motivational Balancing Act

When we describe the research on self-determination theory and achievement goal theory, we often hear practitioners raise questions like, "Encouraging young people to be intrinsically motivated and mastery oriented sounds great, but is it realistic given the fact that many of the reasons for and demands of education are traditionally focused on performance and rewards?" and "Aren't establishing a well-paying career, avoiding poverty, and feeling the pride of one's family legitimate reasons for going to college?" Our answer to these questions is this: adults need to help young people strike a motivational balance.

In order to have the kinds of motivation that will make them most likely to succeed, youth need to have a balance of intrinsic/mastery goals and extrinsic/performance goals, and they need to internalize extrinsic goals so that they feel ownership and purpose in those goals. Practitioners, therefore, need to provide a balanced set of reasons for encouraging young people to go to college and a balanced set of incentives and structures to help them get there. In our experience, college access programs and practices do not often strike this balance. Most rely primarily or solely on extrinsic incentives for attending college, especially financial rewards, and promote performance goals. We are not saying that these kinds of incentives have no role to play in college access. Rather, they should be framed in ways that help students internalize them and utilized in combination with a focus on learning and long-term intrinsic rewards, such as finding an interesting career and making positive contributions to their communities.

Take the case of focusing on the financial rewards of going to college, which practitioners often do by showing youth the chart depicting increases in salary associated with higher educational levels. This is a common strategy, because the financial motive for attaining a college degree is a particularly high priority for first-generation college students, whose financial needs are often more pressing than any other needs. If these financial outcomes are presented as the only reason for college, however, they are likely to have little benefit, or may even be detrimental. This is demonstrated in a study from the Institute for Higher Education Policy that surveyed students who were qualified to get into college but chose not to pursue higher education.[3] Two-thirds of the non-college-goers surveyed agreed with the statement that a college education is necessary for having the things they want, like a car and a nice home. So why didn't they pursue college? The results suggest that one reason was that they didn't engage in the academic preparation necessary. The study's authors interpreted this pattern of results to mean that those students believed going to college wasn't feasible. But the motivation literature suggests another possible explanation (which was not examined in the study): the extrinsic rewards of a college education were not enough to encourage them to do the academic work and take the other steps to apply to and succeed in college.

As another example, several citywide and philanthropic initiatives promote college access by promising scholarships to youth who attain a certain level of academic achievement in high school. These programs are sometimes framed as motivational initiatives, and some schools and communities use them as their only explicit approach to promoting motivation. We believe that these programs can be very valuable—but not as motivational tools. These programs break down barriers to college by providing much-needed financial support, and they can also leverage identity processes by helping youth avoid identity foreclosure caused by the belief that college is financially impossible. But if they are presented as motivational tools, or if they are used with no other psychosocial supports, then they are likely to initiate a problematic motivational cycle. At best, when offered alone with no other support for motivation, they can help young people get to college but then not know why they are there. At worst, they can cause youth to be so focused on the "reward" of getting to college that they lose focus and motivation when they are in college. In contrast, if these kinds of programs are implemented in combination with other strategies that promote intrinsic motivation and mastery-oriented goals, we would expect the results to be very positive.

As both of these examples illustrate, college access efforts should help young people understand the extrinsic aspects of college (such as higher salaries and parents' pride) as being important *in addition to* and *in the service of* intrinsic rewards. They should present young people with a range of reasons for going to college, and these should always include intrinsic reasons, such as finding interesting work and meeting others with similar interests. College access efforts should also help young people find intrinsic interest in some elements of the college planning and preparation process (for example, for some youth this may be writing essays or joining summer programs) and help them to internalize the value of aspects of the college access process that are not inherently rewarding on their own but that lead to fulfillment in the long term.

SUPPORT STRUCTURES FOR SUPPORTIVE GOALS

The messages that adolescents hear about why they should go to college matter, but those messages aren't enough to ensure that youth will develop the kinds of motivation that will help them succeed. Motivation develops in and affects everyday behaviors, and young people therefore need to learn how to set their own mastery-oriented goals and find their own intrinsic motivation in many areas of their lives. While adults can't "give" youth intrinsic motivation or mastery goals, they can work with them in ways that make youth more likely to develop these kinds of goals in their daily lives. Doing so requires understanding the factors that shape intrinsic motivation and mastery orientation. With an understanding of these factors, practitioners can use their everyday interactions with youth to introduce and reinforce the kinds of goals that make young people most likely to aspire to, enroll in, and succeed in college.

Believing That Success Is Controllable

One of the biggest factors that shapes the kinds of goals people set is whether and how people believe that effort influences success. Mastery goals are associated with beliefs that hard work and effort lead to success, whereas performance goals are associated with beliefs that inherent ability is necessary and sufficient for success. This is particularly important when students get to college, because the coursework that they encounter usually requires more effort and time than the high school coursework to which they are accustomed. If students don't believe that more effort will make a difference, they are unlikely to step up their effort and are therefore more likely to struggle academically. This research suggests that it's important for all young people to receive effort-oriented feedback from an early age: "Great job in last night's game! You must be working really hard on your jump shot!" all the way up through the college admissions process through statements such as "This personal reflective essay is very interesting. You must have put a lot of thought into the ideas." It is also important to avoid or moderate the use of ability-focused praise such as "Wow, you got a very high score on the ACT. You must be really smart!" It's also important for them to consistently hear messages about the fact that college is possible through effort and hard work, even in the face of many challenges.

Carol Dweck, one of the developers of achievement goal theory, has shown that whether people set mastery or performance goals is also related to what they believe about intelligence. People who see intelligence as malleable or incremental tend to be oriented toward mastery goals, because they believe that they can always learn more and become smarter. In contrast, those who see intelligence as a fixed entity tend to be oriented toward performing well and demonstrating their ability, because they believe that intelligence is something that you either have or you don't, and they want to prove that they have it or avoid looking like they don't have it.

Theories about the nature of intelligence are not correlated with actual intelligence levels—and they can be changed. Dweck and her colleagues conducted an intervention study in which junior high school students participated in one of two eight-week workshops on the brain and study-skills advice. The key difference between the two workshops was that one taught students to see the brain as a muscle, which can become stronger (to see intelligence as malleable), while the other did not discuss the role of intelligence and focused on memory techniques. At the end of the workshop sessions, the researchers found that students who had been taught that intelligence is malleable were rated by their teachers as engaging in more classroom motivational behaviors (such as putting in more effort and asking for extra help) and displayed a trend toward more mastery-oriented goals and higher grades.[4] These researchers did not follow the students through high school, but Dweck's theories and research suggest that the kinds of outcomes they experienced in middle school would make them more likely to get on and stay on a path to college.

Beliefs about intelligence and effort, while important, are not the only factors that influence how people interpret the causes of their successes and failures. According to attribution theory, people see the reasons for their successes and failures in terms of three primary dimensions, all of which affect their self-efficacy. The first is *locus of control*, which refers to whether people think that their success or failure is due to internal factors over which they have control, or to external factors that are beyond their control. The second factor is *stability*, which refers to whether people believe that the causes of success and failure can change over time. The third is *controllability*, or whether people think that they can change their outcomes through the choices that they make and actions that they take.

Certain combinations of these factors promote more self-efficacy and therefore more success. Whether in education, career, or other domains, people tend to be more successful when they believe that success is internal, controllable, and unstable—that they have the power to influence it and to change it over time. In contrast, when people believe that the reasons for failure are internal, stable, and uncontrollable, they are likely to interpret a failure as deterministic. As a result, they are more likely to be pessimistic and to fall into a learned helpless pattern, making them likely to give up in the face of challenges. In the case of the SAT practice test, Adrian believed in his ability to control the outcome of the SAT and therefore used the first low score as an indication that he needed to work harder before taking the test again. In contrast, Jesse believed that he had low ability and that this ability (which he perceived as uncontrollable) made it impossible for him to succeed; as a result, he believed that there was no point in trying again or in attempting to develop strategies to improve his score.

Practitioners can set youth up for success by helping them develop Adrian's more beneficial pattern of attributions. When young people develop such attributions, they are able to see how their actions affect their outcomes. This empowers them to take responsibility for their academic behaviors, make strong decisions, and cope effectively with the challenges that they will inevitably face. Whether a young person is auditioning for a play, preparing for the SAT, or running a chemistry experiment in a college lab, she is more likely to be successful if she believes the outcome of that activity is something that she can control and that the causes of her success include internal factors such as effort and skill rather than luck or fate. If she performs poorly, she's more likely to persist in the future if she believes that she can effect a different outcome next time and if she understands whether, in addition to effort, some external factors may have been at play, such as the fact that her pencil broke halfway through the SAT, causing her to lose a few moments' focus while finding another one. It is important to discuss young people's previous and upcoming experiences with them in ways that help them think about and interpret the causes of success and failure so that they can develop the attributional patterns that make them most likely to succeed.

Feeling Independent but Connected to Others

One of the things that shapes people's attributions for success and failure, and their motivation in general, is their experience of autonomy. When they feel a sense of control over and self-determination in their work or activities, people are more likely to interpret success and failure in adaptive ways. They are also more likely to be intrinsically motivated. If I feel that running the marathon is my own choice (and that training is an ongoing choice that I make on a weekly basis), I am more likely to find running to be enjoyable and rewarding. But if I run because my doctor prescribed it as part of a weight-loss routine or because I'm being chased by a bear, I will be more likely to focus on getting it done and less likely to enjoy it, and therefore less likely to continue doing it when I have free time and free choice. Situations that provide people with a choice of tasks or methods for completing tasks promote intrinsic motivation, whereas those that are highly controlled by an outsider decrease intrinsic motivation.

This means that young people will be more likely to be intrinsically motivated to go to college and to persist in college if they feel they have choices over whether to go, where to go, which courses to take, and which majors to declare. This is one of the many reasons why practitioners, at both the high school and college levels, need to fully engage adolescents in the process of designing their postsecondary paths and avoid making or pushing certain choices for them. Some well-intentioned practices and policies can reduce young people's perceptions of autonomy and ultimately their desire to go to college. For example, in an attempt to standardize certain college preparatory steps, some schools have begun to require that students complete a college application as part of a class or graduation requirement. Although these strategies strive to reduce the likelihood that some students will fall through the cracks, they also run the risk of making youth feel forced. We have seen some youth resist these efforts, and one reason could be that these youth feel their autonomy has been compromised. They may be rejecting these efforts not because of their purpose, but rather because of their approach. Many of them will likely apply to college anyway, but it is possible that some will become turned off by the entire process. In addition to well-intentioned requirements like these, financial and other extrinsic rewards also exert a form of control. This is one of the reasons that they can actually decrease intrinsic motivation in the long run and why they should be carefully thought out, presented, and balanced with other kinds of encouragement.

Relationships matter for motivation as well. Adolescents are more likely to develop intrinsic motivation when they experience relatedness, when they feel emotionally secure, cared about, and connected to the people around them, especially adult leaders such as teachers and youth workers. Jay, the student who developed a strong desire to go to college through his newfound love of writing, was supported by close relationships with his English teacher and his college student advisor. When young people have this sense of emotional closeness and belonging, they are more likely to internalize the values and rewards promoted by adult leaders and, therefore, to experience extrinsic rewards in the most positive possible ways. In contrast, those who feel a lack of trust in or rejection by those adults are more likely to experience those rewards as purely extrinsic and therefore are less likely to truly integrate the information, values, and goals presented in ways that lead to success. Deci and Ryan, who articulated self-determination theory, have proposed that relatedness provides a foundation for intrinsic motivation in all settings but may be particularly important for tasks that are very challenging, including academic ones. Others have pointed out that relatedness is also particularly important for youth from collectivist cultures, such as Asian and Asian American cultures, which place a high value on the welfare and pride of the group over the individual.

OPPORTUNITIES FOR PRACTICE

Young people's goals, and the factors that shape them, are malleable. Many of the strategies for helping young people develop beneficial goals are not complicated or difficult to implement. Just as motivation is not about quantity but instead about quality, the work of promoting college-going motivation is not necessarily about what adults do with youth but more about how they do it. It is also not something adults can do *to* or *for* youth but, instead, a process in which they must work *with* youth to help them develop their own goals and take agency in achieving them.

Consciously or not, everyone in a young person's life shapes her motivation. Goals are influenced by daily interactions and relationships, both formal, ongoing relationships and casual, short-term relationships. It is therefore important for everyone who works with youth to be intentional and thoughtful about how their messages can influence motivation, in everything from emphasizing mastery goals to encouraging young people to see the value of effort and hard work. Like many other aspects of college preparation, promoting helpful forms of motivation cannot happen exclusively within the walls or hours of a college access program or a student-counselor meeting. For this reason, we present here motivation-supporting strategies that can be embedded into existing daily practices or expanded to form new activities in a range of settings and locations.

Using all of these strategies effectively requires that practitioners be reflective about young people's paths and their own, and about how those paths may differ. This includes understanding the kinds of goals and benefits that first-generation college-bound students perceive as most pressing and important, which may be different from the ones that motivated practitioners at their age. It is important to respect and validate these goals, even the extrinsic and performance-focused ones, while also promoting intrinsic ones and helping young people find a motivational balance.

Specific strategies for shifting the typically limited approach to motivation include the following:

- *When presenting the benefits of college, strike a balance between intrinsic and extrinsic rewards.* Presentations to groups of youth and one-on-one conversations to encourage college-going should mention both extrinsic and intrinsic reasons. To ensure that these messages are consistent, coach speakers and peer mentors who work with youth to provide a balanced set of goals as well. Use extrinsic motivators such as financial rewards sparingly and in combination with intrinsic motivators. For example, stipends and other extrinsic rewards can be valuable for encouraging youth to participate in afterschool and college access programs (especially for removing barriers to participation such as the need to work at a part-time job). But it is important to make those programs engaging and meaningful for youth once there, to help them find parts of the college-going process that are intrinsically interesting (e.g., writing or meeting new people), and to emphasize the intrinsic benefits of higher education.

- *Build on youths' interests and passions to tap into intrinsic motivation for college.* Establishing future-oriented goals that are intrinsically motivating to youth go a long way toward helping them persist in the face of obstacles and maintain a commitment to their college plans. Adolescents know what is important to them, but they may not always draw connections between those things and college. Find out what young people are interested in and intrinsically motivated to do and then help them see how these interests do or can connect to college-going. Through one-on-one conversations, group writing exercises and focus groups, or career interest inventories, help them identify the things that are most interesting and rewarding for them and tailor resources, such as college brochures, campus visits, and internship opportunities.
- *Help young people internalize the benefits of extrinsic rewards and performance goals.* For example, when presenting the salary chart demonstrating the higher-paying careers associated with college degrees, go one step further to discuss how these kinds of careers and the salaries they provide allow people to find meaning in their work, advance up the career ladder so that they can influence the direction of their company or start their own ventures,

and utilize the money they earn to pursue interesting hobbies or contribute to a meaningful charity. As another example, help young people understand how their parents' goals for them and their own desires to make parents proud can provide the encouragement and support to get them on a college-going path that will then allow them develop their own interests and pursue their own passions. Stress how pursuing study and finding a career in these areas can increase the likelihood of their success, which will ultimately make their families and communities even more proud of them. Practitioners can also help young people find their own meaning in performance goals. For example, they can help youth translate a desire to bring pride to their community into pursuing social work, public health, or other fields that will help them give back to their community in ways that are interesting to them and that make them feel good about helping others.

- *Emphasize mastery and learning for academic activities rather than just the end goal.* Through academic work, teachers can help students develop a habit of forming mastery goals that can transfer to college access. Coaches and youth workers can help youth develop similar habits in extracurricular activities. Across settings, adults should help youth see the value of learning for its own sake and for the purpose of pursuing interesting work later by presenting academic content and assignments as interesting, giving young people choices in which topics to pursue or projects to create, and making content relevant and meaningful to their daily lives and their futures. In academic settings, it is also best to avoid performance situations that utilize competition, because when youth compare themselves to one another, they become less focused on the inherent value of the academic material or task and more likely to focus on demonstrating their competence to peers.

- *Stress the value of effort and de-emphasize the role of innate ability in determining success.* Teachers, counselors, youth workers, and all adults can send the important message that young people can always improve by applying more effort. These messages should be reinforced constantly, but windows of opportunities occur before administering tests, before big games or performances, when returning tests and distributing report cards, when revealing results of try-outs and auditions, during planning meetings and goal-setting sessions, and during advisories. It is important to convey these messages before young people engage in academic and planning behaviors to set them up for success. Educators and youth professionals can also become mindful of how to respond when results are disappointing. For example, when we hear youth attribute their successes or failures to things that are not within their control, we must see it as an opportunity to help them reframe their attributional processes. Those who work with youth in athletic programs are especially well positioned to convey these messages and help youth draw connections between goals and skills from athletic settings to academic ones.

- *Help youth find and develop interests and passions.* Finding activities and interests that inspire them can help young people envision specific reasons for and routes to college. These interests can also provide opportunities for youth to develop the experiences of competence and the self-efficacy that support college-going. Youth development programs, extracurricular activities, and internships or part-time jobs provide particularly valuable opportunities for young people to explore and develop these interests, because they are usually voluntary, often allow adolescents some control in how they are organized and run, and provide a needed change of pace from school. However, educators can also provide opportunities for youth to explore their interests during the school day by presenting a wide range of topics and giving students opportunities for choice and control, for example, by allowing them to select their own projects and co-construct classroom policies and syllabi.

6

ORGANIZING

*Realizing College Dreams Through
Self-Regulation*

For even the most intrinsically motivated youth, college access and success require a great deal of organization, planning, and self-management. Throughout the process, college-going requires skills in what researchers call *self-regulation*. Self-regulation is the ability to manage one's thoughts, emotions, and behaviors in the service of attaining goals. Self-regulation encompasses many specific skills, including, but not limited to, the ability to focus attention, plan, delay gratification, solve complex problems, self-reflect, and regulate feelings and social interactions in challenging situations. These skills are essential for academic achievement, which, of course, sets the stage for successfully enrolling and succeeding in college.

But self-regulatory skills also support college-going independent of their effects on classroom behaviors, because they help young people engage in the organizational and planning behaviors necessary for applying to college and for staying the course in the face of difficulties and hardships. Having focus and planning skills helps young people complete applications, manage deadlines, and make plans for paying for college. Having the ability to self-reflect and delay gratification helps them make good choices, both the everyday kind, such as whether to study or hang out with friends the night before a test, and the long-term kind, such as what kind of college programs to apply to.

Unfortunately, these skills are underdeveloped in many young people. As a result, we have seen many youth miss out on opportunities such as college preparatory or other enrichment programs—or miss out on college altogether—because they missed deadlines, put off starting an application, or were simply unable to delay short-term gratification in pursuit of a long-term goal. One reason for this may be that few practitioners, whether teachers, counselors, or youth development workers, are trained to promote these skills. The result is that otherwise beneficial college access efforts do not always achieve their potential, as we have seen in cases like Evelyn's.

At the end of her tenth-grade year, Evelyn's science teacher, Ms. Hoffman, remarked on Evelyn's growth and learning across the academic year. When Ms. Hoffman asked about her future aspirations, Evelyn replied, "Well, I think I'll go to college to become an engineer. I started to really dig science this year." Explaining that taking and scoring well on the SAT would help with college acceptance and perhaps with scholarships, Ms. Hoffman gave Evelyn an SAT practice book and suggested that she work on it over the summer.

But without any strategies or plans for how to use the book or manage her time and responsibilities, Evelyn barely opened the book. With a summer job and a full social calendar, she found little time for it, and when she did glance at it, some of the sections seemed too confusing and difficult, so she tossed it aside and told herself that she'd check it out again later. The fall came quickly, and when there was only a week left before the SAT, Evelyn realized that she hadn't put much time into studying, and she tried to squeeze a few hours of practice in between going to school, working part time, and maintaining her social life. But there was so much material that she didn't even know where to start.

When she returned to school the week after the test, she ran into Ms. Hoffman, who asked, "How did it go?" Evelyn sighed, "I don't think I did very well." When she got her results back, Evelyn saw that she had been right: she had scored only in the twenty-seventh percentile.

Like so many well-meaning adults, Ms. Hoffman set and communicated high educational expectations, affirmed Evelyn's competence in science, helped her establish an intermediate goal, and even gave her a tool to help her achieve that goal. However, Evelyn lacked the self-regulatory skills to effectively use that tool, and she needed more support and structure to develop them. Had Ms. Hoffman or another adult taught her skills in planning and time management and helped her to anticipate and cope with obstacles, Evelyn might have been more engaged over the summer (a typically unstructured and motivationally challenging time) and ultimately been more successful on the test.

Another reason that we have seen good intentions fall short is that many adults engage in practices that actually undermine the development of self-regulatory skills by doing what some youth refer to as "hand-holding." Consider this perspective from a student who struggled in college partly due to a lack of self-regulatory skills: "At high school, they held your hand for everything and didn't teach you how to find resources on your own." This student was one of many quoted in a Boston Higher Education Partnership report about the factors that distinguish students who succeed from those who struggle in or even drop out of college.[1] The report found that many strugglers felt that adults "coddled" them in high school and did not adequately prepare them to assume the levels of responsibility and self-management needed in college. According to one of the reports, "It was striking how many participants, both strugglers and succeeders, remarked that high schools should reduce close adult supervision and instead teach students how to manage school responsibilities on their own."[2]

In all of these cases, adults could have better supported youth by helping them develop the self-regulatory skills necessary to take responsibility for their own future planning. These strategies can make youth more capable of enacting the college-going identities and reaching the goals that we have described in the previous chapters and can also make them more likely to succeed in college, because colleges generally expect students to take responsibility for their own choices and behaviors in everything from selecting courses to regulating their own study behaviors to applying for work study jobs.

In this chapter, you will learn:

- Why self-regulatory skills matter to college access and success
- How adults in a variety of settings can help young people develop these skills not only during college planning and preparation but even (and especially) before

- The role of self-reflection and self-evaluation in helping youth improve their efforts and maximize the likelihood of success
- How to help young people take responsibility for completing college-going tasks

SKILLS FOR TURNING VISION INTO ACTION

Self-regulation is the mechanism that allows people to move from thinking about and hoping for certain outcomes to actually making those things happen. Some researchers have described these skills as "effortful regulation of the self by the self."[3] What this means for college access is that young people with strong self-regulatory behaviors are the masters of their own behaviors and therefore of their destinies. Being in control in this way includes having an active influence over their environments, even as those environments are influencing them.[4] This is important for college access and success because it demonstrates that, even as youths' experiences and futures are being shaped by social factors and educational structures outside of their control, they have the tools and the ability to influence those experiences and in some cases to choose or direct them.

Self-regulatory skills develop gradually over the life span. Very young children begin developing self-regulatory skills by learning to express their needs, self-soothing when upset, and establishing regular patterns of sleeping and eating. In preschool children, self-regulatory development is focused largely on learning to regulate emotions, behave in socially appropriate ways, and develop executive functioning, including paying attention and waiting. Although many people think that self-regulation skills are developed solely during childhood, they continue to develop during and after adolescence. Certain cognitive abilities, such as logical reasoning and information processing, are not fully developed until age fifteen or sixteen, and other cognitive skills such as planning and delaying gratification continue to develop into adulthood. In adolescence and beyond, emerging self-regulatory skills include the ability to solve complex problems and navigate challenging decisions.

Across these ages, people shift not only in what they are learning to regulate but also how. For young children, parents and caretakers are primarily responsible for organizing their time, facilitating their decisions, and regulating their behavior. As children grow, this responsibility slowly shifts away from parents to include influences from peers and ultimately to self-regulation. This development occurs in combination with, and in part because of, the development of neural and biological factors. When middle school and high school practitioners meet them, adolescents have some of the skills that they need to plan for and succeed in college, but they need support from adults to develop the other skills that are continuing or even just beginning to develop. By focusing on and appropriately scaffolding these skills, practitioners can help young people get a head start on where they would be if left on their own. Providing appropriate scaffolding means giving young people tools to help them plan, evaluate decisions, and engage in other important behaviors. Importantly, it means helping them improve and use these tools rather than, at one extreme, doing things for them or hand-holding, or at the other extreme, expecting them to be fully responsible without support.

Like motivation, self-regulation is not something that people have or don't have. All individuals regulate their thoughts and behaviors to some degree, but some are more effective at this than others. And like identity, self-regulation encompasses many specific but interrelated skills. The set of skills that we describe below is not intended to be a full picture of all of the self-regulatory skills that individuals need to succeed, but it focuses on skills that are particularly relevant for college access and success. The skills that we highlight are primarily considered forms of cognitive regulation because they focus on how people regulate their thoughts and other cognitive activities and behaviors. But it is important to note that thoughts, emotions, and behaviors all influence one another and cannot really be separated in practice. Youth who can manage difficult emotions such as frustration and anger are more able to pay attention, make thoughtful decisions, and overcome obstacles. A discussion of youths' skills in managing emotions is beyond the scope of this chapter, but it is an important issue for practitioners to consider.

Focusing and Maintaining Attention

Attention and focus are required for academic success at all levels and are foundational to the other self-regulatory skills that support long-term success. To achieve the goals that they set, people need to be able to focus on information and tasks relevant to the goal while resisting distractions. A common example for elementary school children is listening to the teacher in order to learn how to solve math problems while ignoring other children outside on the playground. Similar skills are needed for college access and success, but they become more complex as youth get older. As every college access professional knows, the simple act of staying on task for completing relevant forms and paperwork for college is common sense, but it's challenging for many youth. Remembering to obtain parent or guardian signatures, returning program paperwork, and recalling which courses are necessary for graduation require that youth manage many distractions and remain focused even when the tasks feel uninteresting.

Maintaining focus is increasingly difficult in our society. At a time when adolescents experience constant interruptions and distractions from television, computer games, social networking sites, text messages, and personal cell phones, we shouldn't be all that surprised when young people struggle to stay on task. Studies show that training programs can help youth with attention and focus (for example, computer training programs have shown promise for helping young people with attention deficit disorder). But adults can also help youth hone their attention skills in simple, everyday ways, both during and well before the college-going process begins. These strategies can include helping young people create dedicated times and places to study and complete applications, teaching them strategies to quiet the mind and focus, and, in the case of parents, helping limit distractions and create "downtime" for the brain to recharge by establishing a no-electronics and no-phone hour before bedtime.

Delaying Gratification

One of the most important, and most challenging, self-regulatory skills for people of all ages is the ability to delay gratification in the interest of long-term goals. We all experience immediate desires, which range from the impulse to open a birthday gift immediately to the desire to eat an entire gallon of ice cream. But people vary in how much they are able to exert control over those impulses in order to do such things as wait until friends can share in the birthday celebration or maintain their weight by eating healthy portions. We often see this difficulty with delaying gratification when young people skip a class to hang out with a friend even though they know that class attendance influences their end-of-semester grade. As psychologist Angela Duckworth has pointed out in her studies of self-regulation, people are often driven to act against their own long-term best interests. In these situations, one decision or behavior is clearly superior to another, but the other is "potent" and difficult to control. This can result in an internal conflict that causes people to do things that may actually keep them from reaching their long-term goals.

The ability to delay gratification is associated with a wide range of positive long-term outcomes, including academic success, less engagement in risky behavior, and better emotional adjustment. In a classic study, Walter Mischel and his colleagues studied young children's ability to delay gratification by using the reward of marshmallows. When a child was brought into the lab, the experimenter placed one marshmallow in front of her, explained that he had to leave the room, and told the child that if she could wait until he returned, she would receive two marshmallows. Some children were able to wait until the experimenter returned and obtained the greater reward of two marshmallows, while others couldn't wait and ate the marshmallow right away or after only a few minutes. Those who had been able to wait used specific strategies, like singing a song to keep themselves busy or looking away from the treat so that they wouldn't become fixated on it. When the researchers followed up with the participants many years later, they found that those who had been able to delay immediate gratification had better self-regulatory skills, did better in school, and had higher SAT scores. Since this experiment, hundreds of research studies have found similar benefits for delay of gratification.

Applying to college requires that adolescents delay gratification in several ways. Most notably, adolescents need to engage in some tasks that are not immediately or inherently rewarding, such as passing a class that feels irrelevant to their future goals or staying after school to receive help with a college essay. But many adolescents struggle with prioritizing behaviors that have long-term benefits but are tedious, uninteresting, or have few clear short-term benefits. For example, SAT preparation is perceived by many youth as tedious and difficult, and many struggle to do it, even though its relevance to future goals is straightforward. Similarly, we remember many young people who never completed scholarship applications despite their concerns for college costs and strong college-going intentions. Sometimes this happens because these tasks compete with activities that are more gratifying in the moment, such as hanging out with friends or playing pick-up basketball. Other times it happens simply because the benefits of the task feel too far in the future; this is one of the reasons that early college awareness and planning activities with middle school youth are challenging.

Practitioners can help young people delay gratification by providing frequent reminders about their long-term college goals and the benefits of those goals. This is particularly important for aspects of the college-going process that have few short-term benefits (such as test taking). In other cases, practitioners can help youth with the parts of the college access process that are intrinsically interesting and motivating, such as writing essays (for those young people who enjoy writing), solving logic problems as part of test preparation (for those who enjoy games), and participating in service-learning programs with friends. They can also include helping youth find programs that match them with paid internships and develop career skills.

Planning and Overcoming Obstacles

The ability to make plans and to organize behaviors in service of those plans is also central to the college-going process. Take, for instance, the need for youth to develop plans for achieving a passing grade on a test. Appropriate strategies might include reviewing class readings, meeting with the teacher, organizing study groups, or taking practice tests. If any of these strategies is ineffective, a young person needs to be able to shift gears and employ an alternative strategy. However, without the ability to think and operate in this way, young people often are left without a plan when their original one fails to work.

C. R. Snyder, a seminal figure in the positive psychology movement, coined the term *pathways thinking* to describe the mental processes that people engage in when they identify specific routes to achieving their goals. This type of planful thinking is part of a process that Snyder refers to as developing *hope*, which he defines as a set of cognitive processes (rather than emotional processes often associated with hope) that work together to get and keep people on track to achieve their goals. According to hope theory, pathways thinking is the catalyst that turns mastery-oriented goals and agency thinking (ownership and responsibility for one's behaviors) into action. For example, a student who aspires to a summer internship at an architecture firm (mastery-oriented goal) has to make a specific plan for writing the essay and sending his transcript and recommendations (pathways thinking), and he also has to feel capable of completing and taking responsibility for those tasks (agency).

One of the important contributions of the pathways thinking concept for college access and success is the focus on *how* people develop and carry out their plans. They do this, in large part, by breaking large goals into subgoals, which are smaller, intermediate goals that can be addressed and accomplished in stages. Snyder has found that people are most likely to engage in hopeful thinking and to ultimately be successful when they set realistic subgoals that are manageable but somewhat challenging—that is, goals that fall somewhere between easily attainable and seemingly impossible. These relatively attainable subgoals build youths' feelings of competence and self-efficacy and keep them on the long-term path.

People are more likely to succeed in achieving their ultimate goals when they set multiple subgoals and envision multiple possible pathways, in case one of the subgoals they have set or routes they have followed becomes blocked. This is particularly important in college access, because there are many ways that a subgoal or route can become blocked, such as a young person not getting a spot in a college access program or not getting accepted to a particular college. If that young person has planned to get all the help he needs from the college access program or has applied to only one college, his future goal of becoming a doctor has quickly become unattainable. In contrast, if he has envisioned many possible routes to his long-term goal (for example, reaching out to adults in his school and community for advice and support and applying to multiple colleges), he will already have a plan B and maybe even a plan C that will keep him on the path.

According to researcher Gabriele Oettingen, another way that individuals stay on the path to their goals even in the face of challenges is through *mental contrasting*. In this process, people envision future goals in the context of current realities, including their challenges and needs. This allows them to be realistic and planful about potential obstacles and to identify strategies for overcoming the obstacles even before the obstacles actually materialize. The case of Nawar, a student with a clear college-bound goal but several challenges, demonstrates how this visualization process can be beneficial.

Nawar was an extremely social and engaged sixteen-year-old who attended a regional urban high school. Due to a learning disability that had been diagnosed at an early age, she received special education services for the majority of her classes but was mainstreamed for two classes. She had always known that she wanted to go to college, and her father had instilled in her the belief that she could do anything she set her mind to, despite her learning challenges.

Nawar knew that she would have to work harder than some of her peers to get the grades and test scores she needed to get into college, so she frequently sought out the support of many people in her school and community. She asked for advice about where she might attend, inquired about the kinds of academic supports available in college, and requested help with her preparation activities. She had an especially positive relationship with the pastor from her church, who had previously worked as a university chaplain and knew a lot about the ins and outs of college admissions and policies. After consulting with him about her college goals, Nawar came to an important realization: based on the way that special education services were organized at her high school, she might not be able to take the classes she needed for college. For example, her need for resource room classes might get in the way of her taking a world language or advanced college preparatory class.

Seeing this potential obstacle, Nawar initiated a meeting with an admissions counselor from a local state college to inquire about admissions requirements. Once she knew what courses were required, she returned to school with the goal of increasing the number of mainstream classes she was taking from two to four. In addition, she requested additional accommodations at her high school and changes to her schedule so that she could take college preparatory courses the following year. Knowing that these classes would be more challenging than the ones she was currently taking and envisioning some academic road bumps, she also requested help from a peer tutor and her pastor so that she could attain the highest grades possible in those courses.

Nawar contemplated how her current reality in special education classes might hinder her admission to college and developed a plan to overcome those challenges to help her reach her goal. Not all youth come to us with these visualization and planning skills fully developed; in fact, this is rare in our experience. One of the reasons that some youth cannot engage effectively in mental contrasting is that they find their current reality too overwhelming and cannot see a different future; educators may see this in youth who dwell on the barriers or the obstacles in the way of college-going. As examples, we have heard adolescents who are parents say that they see having a child as incongruent with going to college, and we have often heard youth from low-income backgrounds say, "I'm too poor to go to college." Oettingen refers to this phenomenon of individuals only considering the negative side of the current reality without taking time to fully envision the desired future goal as *dwelling*. At the other extreme, some individuals focus only on the possible future goal without consideration of potential obstacles, which Oettingen refers to as *indulging*.

Knowing the difference between those who dwell and those who indulge provides a reference point for how to intervene. It is often the case that the young people who readily seek out support from adults are indulgers rather than dwellers. With them, the goal is to assist them in defining potential obstacles, along with positive plans of action for overcoming them, without focusing too much on the negative. In contrast, the dwellers may be tougher to find, because they see their realities as insurmountable and therefore see little value in seeking assistance. With these young people, the goal is first to identify them, then to help them see past the obstacles to envision and elaborate on future goals, and subsequently to help them develop plans for overcoming barriers.

Reflecting and Using Metacognition Skills

One of the processes that enables all of the self-regulatory skills described in this chapter is metacognition, or the process of thinking about one's thoughts. Metacognition allows people to be aware of and thoughtful about how they are approaching their decisions and actions and to create or select strategies best suited to their needs and situations. In turn, this allows them to use and evaluate strategies to remember important information (using a mental picture or a heuristic to remember names of colleges and important application deadlines), to plan (creating a study schedule), and to delay gratification (envisioning long-term benefits, creating visual reminders of those benefits, and finding or creating short-term benefits and incentives). Metacognition also allows people to be self-reflective and to evaluate the outcomes of their decisions and actions and to use that information to revise their approaches in the future.

The benefits of metacognition and self-reflection can be seen in the work of educational researcher Barry Zimmerman, whose model of self-regulated learning illustrates how individuals learn to exert influence and control over learning tasks. Zimmerman's model describes three phases that operate in an ongoing cycle, all of which require or are influenced by thoughtfulness and reflection. We illustrate with a student example:

- The first phase, *forethought*, involves goal setting and planning. *Giovanni aspires to attend a Big Ten school and completes the application because he realizes that it is required in order to be accepted.*
- The second phase, *performance control*, involves observing one's own behavior while engaging in goal-oriented strategies. *While filling out the college application, Giovanni becomes aware that he is skipping a lot of questions that he and his parents do not know how to answer. He makes notes of the questions he needs help with and also highlights areas that require more information.*
- The third phase, *self-reflection*, involves evaluating the experience and making judgments about what worked and what didn't. *On reflection, Giovanni realizes that his decision*

to fill out the application at home made it difficult to complete because his parents were unfamiliar with the process and unable to answer his questions. He decides that he will stay after school and work on it in the college and career center, which will allow him to ask teachers, counselors, or other school staff for help.

Metacognition strongly influences the self-talk and strategies generated in the second phase and the self-assessments and judgments in the third phase, which ultimately inform future planning and action and therefore fuel the entire regulatory cycle. Just as these skills can help young people learn new information, they can help youth make college-going decisions and engage in the behaviors to enact those decisions. For example, a student who decides to improve her SAT performance might use this process to identify study strategies.

MEETING YOUTH HALFWAY

While all of this research demonstrates how important self-regulation is for college access and success, its role has historically been invisible to many of the people who work with youth. In our experience, many practitioners do not think about whether young people have the skills necessary to organize their time, manage distractions, navigate strong emotions, or engage in the other self-regulatory skills and behaviors we have described. Some of these practitioners assume that young people already have these skills and don't need to be taught. Making matters more challenging, educational institutions and policies do not prioritize these skills for either young people or adults: young people's self-regulatory skills are not measured or evaluated for high school degree completion or college admissions, and preservice and in-service programs for counselors, teachers, and other practitioners rarely discuss why these skills matter or how to support them.

As a result of these factors, we often see well-meaning adults take on many of the responsibilities of college planning and preparation rather than helping youth develop the self-regulatory skills to complete these tasks themselves. Some are so adept at creating organizational systems for application materials that their students have no need to develop these skills for themselves. Like "helicopter parents," some practitioners or mentors may believe that they are acting in young people's best interests when they complete tasks for them rather than risking that the tasks go uncompleted. This was the case for the well-meaning college student that one of us once found writing a college essay for a high school senior.

Scaffolding self-regulatory skills is a vital part of helping young people be successful before, during, and after college. Self-regulatory skills help young people own the college-going process and complete the necessary steps more successfully. These skills also help them develop the internal capacity to benefit from other college access services and supports. In addition, the self-regulatory skills that promote college-going play a central role in college-staying. Colleges have fewer structures to help students stay organized and focused than high schools, and, as a result, students need to have those skills as soon as they arrive on campus.

Supporting the development of self-regulatory skills is important for all young people, but it is particularly important for first-generation college-bound youth. Many of these youth, especially those from low-income and immigrant families, have to navigate many competing demands, such as part-time jobs, and family responsibilities, such as translating for parents and taking care of younger siblings, all while keeping up with their schoolwork and applying to college. Unfortunately, these competing demands mean that the college-going process can require even more planning and time management skills for these youth than for their more advantaged peers. Delaying gratification may be particularly challenging for these youth as well, partially because immediate needs like financial stresses are so pressing and partially because many of their peers and community members may not be engaged in the kind of future planning that they are.

At the same time, many first-generation college-bound youth have promising opportunities to develop their self-regulatory skills that their peers may not have. For instance, because many (although certainly not all) first-generation students are from families facing economic stresses, many of them have part-time jobs to help support their families or to prepare for their futures. These jobs require that youth plan their schedules, meet timelines, arrange transportation, and control immediate desires and impulses while in the work setting. Similarly, youth from immigrant families often have substantial responsibilities at home—helping to run family businesses and/or taking care of younger siblings—that require them to make clear-headed decisions, be focused, and multitask. We have often heard young people with these kinds of job and family responsibilities say that they "like to be busy," partly because it helps them manage their time and be organized. But many practitioners may not recognize these responsibilities as opportunities for skill development and miss the chance to help youth make connections between the skills they are learning at home and in the workplace and those required for college.

It is important to note that helping youth engage in self-regulated behaviors is not the same thing as leaving them to their own devices with no support. To illustrate, we describe a compromise that Mandy struck when she was a school counselor working with many first-generation college-bound youth.

After working hard to complete applications for scholarships, the FAFSA (Federal Application for Free Student Aid), and college admissions, many of my students were failing to put those applications in the mail. During my first year, I watched too many promising students miss out on opportunities as a result. In my second year, as the deadlines for applications approached, I would lay awake in bed and wonder, "How can I prevent this from happening again?" The easiest option would have been to send the application forms myself. But I knew that this would undermine all of my other efforts to teach students to take responsibility for their own paths.

After wrestling with the issue for weeks, I finally hit on a compromise: I bought a roll of stamps and sold them to students in my office. With the mail basket in the main office, this system allowed them to take ownership of the process but removed what had been yet one more hurdle for some of them—getting a stamp.

We recognize that it can feel risky to ask young people to take responsibility for aspects of the college-going process, because the stakes of youths' futures are so high. This is why it is so important to find compromises like this one that scaffold young people's self-regulatory skills.

OPPORTUNITIES FOR PRACTICE

Scaffolding self-regulatory skills can take time, especially because practitioners often need to develop their own strategies that work best for their populations' unique situations. We recognize that adding these strategies to already-heavy workloads can be challenging and that smoothing the path is sometimes easier than teaching youth the skills to walk the path themselves. But taking that time and making the effort can save time and trouble in the long run, both for practitioners and, more importantly, for youth. The following strategies provide some ideas that practitioners in a variety of roles and settings can employ or use as inspiration for creating their own approaches.

- *Teach self-regulatory skills.* Use advisories, ninth-grade academies, and senior seminars to explicitly teach self-regulatory skills such as how to plan ahead, manage time, evaluate decisions, and reflect on the outcomes of decisions in order to improve performance. Remember that youth do not necessarily have fully developed self-regulatory skills and that schools, youth programs, and college access programs are ideal settings for introducing and practicing these skills. Give youth specific tools such as planners, calendars, questions to consider when making decisions, and strategies for making pros-and-cons lists. These skills can be taught in the context of assignments for other classes (e.g., math or science) and then can be reinforced by applying them to college-going processes. With this kind of reinforcement, these skills have the potential to become habit-forming behaviors, and youth will become accustomed to using them by the time they have to engage in the complex, sometimes tedious tasks required for college planning and preparation.

- *Provide strategies to help youth minimize distractions.* Enhancing self-regulatory skills includes providing support for the development of attention and focus. Help youth develop these skills by frequently reinforcing their importance, asking them to brainstorm strategies for maintaining focus, and suggesting strategies such as creating dedicated time and space at home or in community settings (e.g., libraries) to complete the tasks required for college-going. Teach simple strategies that can be used in any setting to refocus in the face of distractions, such as closing eyes and taking deep breaths, journaling to clear the mind of other thoughts, and visualizing images that bring to mind a state of calm.

- *Help youth keep their eyes on the prize while also finding short-term benefits and interests in the college-going process.* Delaying gratification can be challenging, especially for younger youth just beginning to plan for college. This is due in part to the fact that college-going goals are sometimes distant, and youth struggle to find meaning in the sub-goals associated with planning and preparing for college. Help bring the long-term benefits into reach by providing frequent reminders of them and making them as tangible as possible. For example, engage college graduate mentors and speakers to whom youth can relate and ask them to help youth see connections between the long-term payoffs of college and their current interests. At the same time, help youth find elements of the college preparation and planning process that are meaningful and rewarding in the short term, anything from interesting courses to enrichment programs to exciting field trips. Help youth develop concrete subgoals and help them write them down or make visual reminders of them. Just as importantly, help them see their progress toward those goals. For example, encourage them to create visual representations (like a picture of a thermometer or a timeline with checkmarks for items already completed) and identify opportunities to celebrate the achievement of subgoals. With all of these activities, it is important to emphasize relevance by structuring them in ways that are relevant to youths' current and future lives and that help youth see this relevance.

- *Teach youth to become adept at developing alternative plans or multiple pathways.* It is important that youth see multiple routes to the same goal, including the ultimate goal of attending college and subgoals such as taking on leadership roles, enrolling in challenging classes, and developing relationships with adults who can provide support. Through individual advising or goal-setting workshops, encourage young people to be open-minded and creative about the pathways for reaching their goals and suggest subgoals that they may not have considered. A suggestion for teaching these skills is to conduct exercises in which young people set a goal and then identify at least three paths to that goal, similar to the way that Google Maps or other GPS devices offer more than one route to a geographic destination in case the driver encounters traffic or road work. (In fact, this visual metaphor can be used in exercises to help make the process visible and tangible for young people.)
- *Help youth identify potential barriers and obstacles and develop strategies for overcoming them.* Use brainstorming exercises

167

in group counseling or other group settings to expand youths' repertoires of strategies for overcoming setbacks. The group conversation allows youth to hear the strategies of their peers and therefore expand their own repertoire of options. Another way to do this is by integrating "if then" strategies into classroom curricula and goal-setting activities. Through these strategies, youth begin to envision possible scenarios and outcomes and make a plan matched to each of them. This can be particularly important at key transition points (pre-summer vacation or precollege enrollment), which tend to be vulnerable times for maintaining self-regulation and achieving goals. Before and during these transition times, ask youth to identify one to three potential barriers that might get in the way of a previously established goal, and then ask them to create a plan for overcoming each.

- *Teach self-regulatory skills in academic courses and help students transfer them to college-going.* One strategy is to use an approach created by Zimmerman and his colleagues in which teachers use the cycle of self-regulated learning that we described earlier to solve academic problems or exercises. Youth define a problem (set a goal or plan), develop strategies to address the problem (performance), and assess the effectiveness of their actions (self-reflection). This cycle is mostly about reflection that informs future behaviors, something that can be used in most everyday practices. Teachers can apply a similar approach in their own lesson planning in order to model this process for students. To do so, they structure tasks around planning (forethought), solving problems (performance control), and then assessing the effectiveness (self-reflection).

- *Encourage youth development programs and employers to emphasize self-regulatory skills.* Youth development practitioners are particularly well positioned to help youth make the connections between self-regulatory skills and how those skills develop in the workplace, because their programs often include opportunities for youth to plan their own projects, participate in internships, and conduct community service. These kinds of real-world experiences require youth to develop and apply many of the self-regulatory skills described in this chapter. They also provide youth with more chances to make choices and express their voices than do traditional classroom activities, and these kinds of opportunities are essential for helping youth learn to take responsibility. By taking a few extra minutes to talk with youth about their developing self-regulatory skills, program leaders can help young people understand the importance of these skills, develop the capacity for self-reflection and other metacognitive strategies, and transfer them to college access and success.

7

CONNECTING

Marshaling the Support of Peers and Families

From envisioning a college-going path to planning the route for getting there, young people need to be active agents in every stage of the process. But this doesn't mean that they can or should approach college-going alone. Supportive relationships with others in their families, schools, and communities are essential for college access and success, in part because these relationships support the processes of identity, motivation, and self-regulation that we've described in previous chapters. In other words, young people need to be connected in order to become independent.

Research shows that children and adolescents are more likely to be well-adjusted and successful when they have even one strong relationship with an adult or one good friend, but it also shows that the more connections and social supports the better. These principles apply to college-going as well. Parents, extended family members, peers, community members, mentors, and employers can all make a difference in college-going. School and program staff offer valuable support, but they can do more and see better outcomes for youth when they marshal the support of other key people for at least three reasons. First, counselors and other college access professionals have very high caseloads, and even the most dedicated among them often struggle to reach all young people. Second, peers and adults who interact with youth outside of school are often well-positioned to reach those youth (sometimes more so than educators) because of their close relationships, frequency of contact, and lack of power differentials that exist between educators and youth. Third, because the developmental processes occur in multiple settings and over time, they require ongoing efforts from all of the people who touch youths' lives.

However, the resources of families, peers, and community members often go untapped by school counselors, college access professionals, and policy makers. Ironically, one of the reasons that we've seen this happen comes from practitioners' desire to help. Most people who work with youth entered their professions to help others, but sometimes the desire to feel useful or to make a big difference gets in the way of engaging the support of others. In some cases, this occurs because funders or policy makers want organizations to demonstrate that they have made a unique and measurable impact; these situations can unintentionally create incentives for practitioners *not* to collaborate. In other cases, this occurs because caring adults simply aren't aware of what other people have to offer or, more concerning, they don't trust them.

Lack of trust is rarely stated overtly. More often, it is conveyed subtly, in the form of the deficit-focused approach that many practitioners take when it comes to youths' social relationships. Many programs frame their work as counteracting negative peer influences or compensating for family deficits. Demonstrating this trend, an article in a major newspaper that profiled a community-based college access program described counselors as filling the shoes of parents and compensating for their lack of "knowhow." It aimed to demonstrate the important role that college access professionals play, but it did so in a way that suggested that parents, and low-income parents in particular, are deficient. It revealed the kind of implicit classism and racism that are not uncommon in schools and community programs serving first-generation college-bound students, and it failed to see the many ways that parents from all social classes, races, and cultural groups positively influence student success.

Whether this deficit-focused perspective came from the reporter or from the college access program itself, it is not unusual in practice. And it is unfortunate, because it marginalizes parents, creates distance between young people and the well-intentioned professionals who aim to support them, and misses a crucial opportunity. By definition, working with first-generation college-bound students is about setting them on a path of which their families, and maybe friends, have little or no experience. However, families and friends have many other assets to offer to support the college-going processes described in this book—especially when practitioners create opportunities to leverage those assets.

Creating these opportunities requires that college access efforts move beyond their traditional approaches, which focus primarily on social capital, or information sharing, that occurs in relationships. In college access, this usually takes the form of adults (especially counselors and mentors) providing information to youth and sometimes families about college requirements, costs, and related knowledge. But relationships can also support other vital developmental processes and, in so doing, provide additional support for college-going.

We focus here on two types of relationships that we see as underutilized sources of support in college access and success: peers and families. Of course, many other people also matter in promoting college access and success. However, we see engaging peers and families as a useful and valuable place for practitioners to start, and from which they can apply many of the processes and strategies we describe here to working with other adults, such as mentors, community members, and other school staff not traditionally associated with college access. We describe how relationships with these people can support the processes of identity, self-concept, motivation, and self-regulation described in earlier chapters.

In this chapter you will learn:

- How peers can positively influence youths' college-going behaviors
- How practitioners can capitalize on peer group dynamics by working with cohorts or small groups of youth
- Why involving families in college access can and should include more than sharing information
- How cultural differences and mistrust between schools and families can obscure the valuable contributions that families make
- How practitioners can begin to move beyond these barriers and work more effectively with families

THE POWER OF PEERS

Anyone who spends time with adolescents knows that peers play a central role in their lives, influencing a wide range of decisions and behaviors. Educators, parents, and researchers often focus on the potentially negative roles of peer influence, such as peer pressure in substance use. But peers can have a positive influence as well, as was the case for Tola and Jessenia.

During high school, Jessenia and Tola were best friends. Having known each other since middle school, they took most of the same courses and excelled in school. Both academically engaged, they regularly participated in extracurricular and enrichment activities, they studied together for tests, consulted one another on topics for class projects, and took turns providing motivational pep talks when one experienced a setback of some sort.

Throughout high school, Jessenia and Tola talked extensively about going to college and supported one another's college-going plans by working together to select a college major, identify a list of colleges, and remind one another of impending deadlines.

Despite having spent so much time together in high school, they headed to different colleges, Jessenia to study nursing and Tola to study psychology. Tola had been away from home before to attend a summer program, but Jessenia had not, and she had never spent more than a few days away from her boyfriend, Brandon, with whom she had been serious for almost two years and hoped to marry.

During their first year of college, the two young women talked often and even visited each other on occasion. During a fall visit, Jessenia told Tola that her courses were going well but that she struggled with unease at school and conflicting desires about her path. "I think I want to have a baby with Brandon," she said. "I

miss him so much when I'm at school, even though I go home ev-
ery weekend to see him and know we'll get married someday. I
just feel better around him than anyone else, and I just don't feel
like myself at college." Tola was shocked. "What are you talking
about?" she asked, taking Jessenia's hands. "After all we've been
through, planning and working and all. To throw it all away to
have a baby right now, that's crazy."

Deep down, Jessenia believed that Tola was right, but she had
another reason for wanting to have a baby that she was reluctant
to share with Tola: she was afraid that Brandon wouldn't wait
for her while she was at college and that he might meet someone
else. The more she talked to her best friend, Jessenia realized that
Brandon wasn't the only one she was missing: she also missed hav-
ing face-to-face contact with a friend and academic partner, some-
one who could keep her on track, encourage her, and push her, like
she and Jessenia had done for one another in high school.

It turned out that Tola missed this, too. Before Jessenia went
back to her own campus, she and Tola made a plan: they would
use texting to send one another reminders about the importance
of school and talk each Sunday night when Jessenia was the most
homesick, and Jessenia would talk to Brandon about her concerns.

When Jessenia opened up to Brandon about her fear of los-
ing him, he reacted in a way that surprised her. Brandon told
her that, while he missed her, he loved that she was in college and
said, "I want my girl to get her education. Babies can wait . . . but
we'll sure have lots of them later." With this extra support from
Brandon, and with Tola checking on her and providing constant
reminders of their shared goals, Jessenia began to settle into her
role as a college student. She even began to associate with new
friends and classmates, something she hadn't even realized that
she had failed to do earlier in the semester.

❖ ❖ ❖

Many youth may not be aware of the many ways in which their peers can positively shape and support their postsecondary paths. And because adults are often unaware of these influences too, most college access efforts place little or no focus on peers, whether in one-on-one relationships or in groups. Yet, in Jessenia's case, both Tola and Brandon were instrumental in supporting her identity as a college student and her ability to stay focused on her college-going goals.

In contrast to college access, research on peer relationships has had a big influence on other fields like youth development programming, the arts, and even health. This research has shown that the influence of peers includes, but is not confined to, friendships and other one-on-one relationships. New methods designed to study group dynamics have quantified the power of peer networks, defined as people who voluntarily interact in identifiable patterns and have some degree of influence over one another. In their book *Connected: The Surprising Power of Our Social Networks and How They Shape Our Lives*, researchers Nicholas Christakis and James Fowler showed that obesity and other health outcomes can be predicted by social influences, including not only one's friends but friends of friends.[1] Their study showed that it is important to think about broad social contexts. Developmental psychologists are now taking a similar perspective and using similar methods to study peer networks in schools and other youth settings. They are finding that peer networks establish norms and influences that are distinct from those of individual relationships; in other words, the whole of the peer group is bigger than the sum of its parts. While the power of the group can sometimes magnify detrimental norms, as sometimes happens in cases of bullying and substance use, it can also bolster positive norms, such as working hard in school and going to college.

Because peers play such a large role in the lives of young people, understanding the positive roles they can play in college access—including the role of individual friends and of larger peer groups—is an important and often missed opportunity. Indeed, some studies have found that urban, minority youth are more likely to enroll in college when they have friends who wish for them to go to college and when their friends are also making plans to go college. One study even found that youth who are surrounded primarily by peers who are going to college are four times more likely to enroll themselves than youth with no friends going to college.[2]

Finding these supports is not necessarily easy. Many first-generation college students are enrolled in schools or live in neighborhoods where few of their peers go to college. This doesn't mean that they don't have access to peer support but, instead, that they may not have access to a broad network of peer modeling, goal sharing, or social capital for college. Compounding the problem, though, is the fact that most educators have been led to believe that the *only* influence peers have is negative, and they have not seen the opportunities that *do* exist to build on positive influences. Our goal here is to illuminate these opportunities and how to capitalize on them, drawing on research that has rarely been applied in this context.

Peers as Mirrors

Peers play a large role in whether youth form college-going identities. As we described in chapter 3, identity development occurs not in isolation but within social relationships. Youth come to define themselves partially through the groups in which they are members. As a result, they are more likely to behave in ways that they see other people "like them" behaving. When it comes to college access, this means that young people are more likely to aspire to and attend college if they see other members of the groups with which they identify going to college. In this process, older mentors or adult community members who have graduated from college can help youth define themselves as college-goers. But because peers are particularly salient during adolescence, it can be particularly beneficial for young people to see others their own age who aspire to college and who share their race, class, sexual orientation, or extracurricular interests.

Some programs and practices intentionally leverage this by creating ethnically, racially, or economically similar groups of youth (and then also matching them with program leaders from similar backgrounds), partially to encourage youth to reach out for support as needed. For example, a Level Playing Field Institute report showed that many programs designed to support the college enrollment and retention of African American males are strategically made up of African American male peer groups and mentors who provide emotional and social support.[3] In some cases, these young men reported that this peer support enabled them to take risks they may not have taken otherwise. Similarly, research finds that African American and Latino college students prefer this kind of peer support over professional services when it comes to coping with the transition into college and establishing and maintaining study skills, jobs, and career aspirations.[4]

College access programs can also capitalize on positive peer influence by setting the context for conversations among peers that allow youth to explore how to honor one's culture while addressing the barriers to college-going. According to one practitioner, these types of conversations, even among peers close in age, can be very powerful:

> My ninth-grade students participate in a great program with a university about an hour away. The students have a chance to really get to know the college kids, hear about their backgrounds, and gain an understanding of their own paths to college. There is always a big cookout where the high school students and college students come together to talk about issues of identity, social class, opportunity structures, and various paths to college admissions, financing, and persistence. Even though the high school students are only freshmen, the fact that these conversations are grounded in actual relationships with the college students allows them to really think about their own paths and picture themselves in college.

Peers as Companions

Young people behave like their friends not just because they believe that this is what "people like me" do, but also because they want to fit in. Most youth have a strong desire to feel a sense of belonging and strong desires to conform to social norms, especially those set by friends and by peers who are perceived to be leaders. As a result, peer modeling can be very influential. Just as peers' risk-taking behaviors and engagement in popular culture can influence young people's choices about whether to drink and whether to listen to certain music, their college-going decisions and behaviors can similarly shape behaviors. Social norms that emphasize college-going can be very powerful, and this is one of the reasons that many schools now aim to promote college-going cultures that stress shared norms and expectations for college-going.

Most youth also want to be in situations that will allow them to spend time with their friends, as was the case with Savannah, the young woman we introduced in chapter 3. Savannah chose an afterschool job at the mall over a college access program because of her desire to be with friends, but if her friends had been participating in the program, she probably would have made the alternative decision. Similarly, young people may be more likely to go to college if their friends are also going to go to college. Even attending different colleges may allow them to share experiences and continue to relate to one another, as was the case with Jessenia and Tola. Similarly, young people will likely be more motivated to participate in college-focused afterschool programs or take college preparatory classes if their friends are also participating. Capitalizing on this desire for time with friends, afterschool programs designed for middle school youth sometimes recruit groups of friends to join together. Many have found this to be an effective strategy for recruiting adolescents into their programs at a time when participation tends to wane in the face of competing desires to hang out with friends in unstructured settings and take on part-time work.

Even beyond reaching out to a few friends, we believe that if practitioners are to be truly successful in reaching all youth, they need to influence the values, goals, and dynamics of entire peer groups. One way to do this is by working with large groups or even entire cohorts of youth. While few college access efforts have made peer influence a major focus, the Posse Foundation has employed a successful group-based strategy.

The Posse Foundation is a youth leadership development and college diversity program that selects small cohorts ("posses") of highly qualified low-income urban students and connects them with selective colleges and universities. The ten-person posses gather in structured and unstructured meetings to support one another before, during, and after the transition to and through a selective university. (Posse Scholars also receive scholarships.) The peer group component is most pronounced in the eight-month precollegiate training program, during which Posse Scholars engage in team building, cross-cultural communication, and leadership development activities. Through these activities, the program creates a cohort in which the youth provide one another with—and presumably benefit from—social, academic, and interpersonal support.

Peers as Regulators

Jessenia's story illustrates how peers can also play a role in helping youth regulate their own behaviors. Although Jessenia was probably unaware of it, her academic and college planning behaviors were being informed by Tola's behaviors and encouragement, and chances are that Jessenia was playing a similar part for Tola. That peers would play such a central role in helping youth regulate their behavior (for example, by creating study plans, structuring how they approach assignments, and coorganizing the college application process), is not all that surprising. As we described in chapter 5, although young people need to have self-regulation skills—they need to be able to manage their own thoughts, emotions, and behavior in ways that prepare them for college—these skills develop in relationships with other people. Before a person can engage in self-regulation, he engages in *other regulation*, in which significant others provide valuable information about and structure for how to behave. Peers are an especially important source of other regulation in adolescence.

In college access, peers can provide a form of other regulation by establishing norms for college-going and for the habits necessary to get to college and persist once there (such as participating in college preparation programs, setting goals and focusing on them, and maintaining high grades even when it means missing out on fun events in order to study). These values and behaviors can set up social expectations that are then internalized and translated into self-regulatory behaviors. As a bonus, peers' academic and college-going behaviors can also provide information and instrumental support, which reinforce and support college-going values and norms and which may be particularly valuable for first-generation college-bound youth. With the growth of social media, there are numerous ways for peers to provide other regulation and to support its translation into self-regulation. For instance, by simply posting about their academic and college-related activities on Facebook and other social networking sites, youth may subtly remind and encourage their peers to engage in similar behaviors. Practitioners can help facilitate this process of peer regulation through creating opportunities for youth to work together in groups, matching students with peer advisors and study partners, engaging the use of social media, and employing the kinds of strategies we will describe. They can also fully embrace the power of peers and the importance of agency by involving youth in creating these activities. Most youth naturally gravitate toward their peers, and youth are quite savvy about how to engage their friends, so we suggest that educators invite youth themselves to come up with ways to support peer programming. We imagine that they will have some creative ideas that we adults couldn't dream of.

OPPORTUNITIES FOR PRACTICE

Whether in schools or in community-based programs, peer-focused strategies can be added relatively easily to existing offerings, and while some may require new resources, others mostly require reorganizing existing structures, which may even result in consolidating resources and effort. Research on and intentional practices for leveraging peer influence are growing but are still new. As the knowledge base grows, here are a few approaches to try:

- *Ask youth about their friends' aspirations and plans.* While it may seem logical to adults that youths' friends influence their goals and behaviors, this process may be subconscious for youth. Help make this process conscious by helping youth identify which friends are thinking about college. In one-on-one conversations, ask questions. And use group settings such as youth programs and group counseling to facilitate discussions about aspirations, expectations, and goals, because hearing peers' thoughts and plans might help some youth reinforce their goals, consider new ideas, and build confidence in striving for their goals. Once youth are in the planning and applying stages of college access, encourage them to work with partners to share their hopes and plans, visit colleges together, or work on application forms together. College access programs might host a "bring a friend" day, where youth can bring anyone to participate and counselors and youth workers can reach out to youths' families to encourage them to schedule college visits together.

- *Create structures for peer-oriented and peer-directed college planning.* Because of the salience of identity and the role of peer regulation in college access, adolescents can benefit from relationships with peer advisors, or "near peers" (those who are close in age but slightly older and usually already in or graduates of college). This can be especially powerful when youth and these peer advisors share elements of their identities, such as cultural backgrounds, home neighborhoods, or high schools. But many adolescents may be reluctant to seek out support from peers on their own. It is therefore important for adults to provide the structure for adolescents to build these relationships. This can include peer group advisories in which youth collaboratively explore their identities, set goals, and identify and address both opportunities and potential barriers. It can also include peer college advising programs, which usually match a high school student and a college student. In a less programmatic approach, practitioners can employ social media as a tool for facilitating discussions about future plans and can increase the likelihood of rich discussion by identifying an "ambassador" youth from a college access program or advisory group to instigate and continue the discussions.

- *Facilitate peer study groups and group projects.* Peer study groups linked to school courses are similar to discussion sections for college courses in which a teaching assistant facilitates discussion, shared work, or extra support among a small group of students outside of class time. Group projects, which can be specifically focused on exploring college opportunities or more generally used to support academic work, also provide opportunities to capitalize on the peer processes described earlier. Educators have long agreed that collaborative learning experiences make for good pedagogy, and they can also make for strong postsecondary paths.

- *Include activities that capitalize on specific cultural identities that support college-going.* Building on the fact that cultural identity is a strong influence on many adolescents' college-going identities and choices, provide opportunities during group discussions or goal-setting workshops for youth to hear from their peers about how their future goals align with their cultural traditions and values. This might include inviting youth to talk about how obtaining a college degree can help them contribute to their communities or hosting recent graduates to speak and coaching them to focus on issues related to community, culture, and aspects of their identity. Once youth are preparing to begin college, it can also be helpful for both high school and college level counselors and administrators to encourage them to seek out other students on campus who share their ethnic and cultural backgrounds.

- *Create opportunities to build networks among youth bound for the same colleges or types of programs.* Because adolescents sometimes struggle to find peers who share their academic pursuits or goals, especially if they live in communities or attend schools with low college-going rates, practitioners can act as brokers to help youth find or

186

create supportive peer communities. During high school, practitioners can help youth connect with peers planning to pursue the same types of programs (e.g., pre-med or journalism) or types of schools (e.g., large university or small college). They can do this by creating programs and lunchtime or afterschool groups or, informally, by connecting youth with one another. During the summer before college entrance, adults can use similar methods to help youth begin to build relationships with others planning to attend the same colleges. College administrators play an important role in this strategy: for example, through "summer bridge" programs that provide academic support, or orientation events that provide, in part, social support. Another strategy is to focus efforts such as recruitment into college access programs on young people perceived to be peer leaders and then working with them to involve other young people.

- *Ensure that programs based on an intentional cohort model include explicit programming to leverage peer resources.* Many college access programs, such as GEAR UP, are based on a cohort model (working with groups or even entire grade levels) using a group structure that inherently creates interactions among peers. However, these programs have rarely included activities that are designed or framed specifically to capitalize on the power of peers. For example, many programs use cohort models because of the potential for youth to share information and resources with one another, but without formal structures to facilitate that exchange, it is unlikely to occur. These programs can more intentionally capitalize on the role of peers by first utilizing team- and community-building activities (such as getting-to-know-you games, trust games, and opportunities to share personal experiences and values), and then intentionally incorporating the other activities described here and being explicit with youth about their goals.

THE MULTIPLE FACETS OF FAMILY SUPPORT

Given the important role of peers, many people think that families have less influence during adolescence than at earlier ages. However, it would be more accurate to say that families' influences change during adolescence, becoming less focused on providing direct, instrumental support and more focused on providing structure and guidance, including helping young people begin to prepare themselves for independent futures. Families play a very important role in determining young people's postsecondary paths. In fact, families may be the single most important influence on youths' college-going and career planning. One study found that an overwhelming 88 percent of adolescents shared their parents' beliefs about the types of occupations they consider acceptable and the kinds of preparation needed for those occupations.[5]

In college access efforts today, much of the attention to families has focused on the role of socioeconomic status and the detrimental effects of lack of financial and educational capital in families with low incomes and/or little education. And while many college access programs strive to involve families, the focus of this work has been limited to two primary pathways: helping families build college-going aspirations and giving families information that they can use to help their children realize those aspirations by helping with the procedural aspects of college preparation. Focusing on these pathways makes some sense, because research shows that expectations are one of the most powerful ways that families influence their children's high school achievement and college aspirations.

However, families can and do support college-going in many other ways as well, notably through supporting the other developmental processes we have described in this book. For example, some of the most effective ways that families can support college access include helping their children be organized, setting aside dedicated time and space for academic and college-related activities, and being intentional and planful about the future. Focusing on these roles represents a paradigm shift for many practitioners, because when educators and other professionals hear "family involvement," they often think of parents showing up at school-based events and attending meetings at community programs. (While many researchers use the term *parental involvement*, we prefer the more inclusive *family involvement* because it includes all of the adults who fill parental roles including grandparents, aunts, and uncles as well as foster parents and guardians.)

Although it is often difficult for those who work in schools and community settings to see these other ways that families influence their children's academic and postsecondary success, understanding them is crucially important, both to gain a deeper understanding of youths' lives and to build on positive family influences in order to make an even bigger difference for youth. We are not proposing that it is the role of practitioners to shape adolescents' relationships with their families, but rather that it is their responsibility to understand families, respect them, and build meaningful relationships with them.

Scaffolding Self-Regulation

Just like peers, families can support college access and success in part through providing structure and support that builds adolescents' self-regulation, including academic habits and future planning. Families can help their adolescent children by teaching them time management, by creating a dedicated space for homework, and by asking probing questions about what they are learning in school, extracurricular activities, and part-time jobs and about how this learning applies to their lives and futures. The Harvard Family Research Project, which has identified three categories of family involvement in education, classifies these sorts of activities as *responsibility for learning*. (The other two categories of family involvement are *supportive parenting* and *home-school relationships*.) We see this term as particularly apt for adolescents, because it underscores both families' responsibilities and their roles in helping their children assume responsibility for themselves.

Responsibility for learning appears to be one of the most effective types of involvement for families of adolescents. A combined analysis of more than fifty studies on middle school students found that the type of family involvement mostly strongly linked to achievement and postsecondary success was *academic socialization*, the category that included families discussing learning strategies, making preparations for the future, communicating about the value of education, and linking schoolwork to current events and students' futures.[6]

Responsibility for learning is also one of the most common and most appropriate forms of educational involvement among families of adolescents, in part because it strikes a developmentally appropriate balance of providing both support and a degree of independence. This is especially useful in light of adolescents' need to find a balance between connectedness to and autonomy from others, especially adults.[7] Because adolescents are becoming more independent, and because college is inherently about taking responsibility for one's own future, families need to provide support in ways that respect and build that independence and that do not feel intrusive or interfere with youths' own decision making.

Much of what we know about autonomy-supportive family involvement comes from research on homework, which finds a logical but sometimes overlooked pattern: when parents help students in ways that are supportive and promote their autonomy, students complete more and better homework, but when parents are overly involved or intrusive, students feel less competent, more negative about school, less engaged in their schoolwork, and more anxious. Autonomy-supportive homework practices, which include providing an organized place to do homework, helping students find or borrow necessary materials, and checking in without nagging or supervising, are the same kinds of things that parents can do to support college access. Other appropriate strategies can include encouraging their children to take the SAT/ACT, helping them brainstorm college essay topics, and accompanying them on college visits (but allowing young people to do the talking). What is important is that parents be involved but not become helicopter parents who complete college applications or sit in on interviews.

Strategies that fall into the category of responsibility for learning are not only developmentally appropriate but are also most doable for families. In contrast, many families find it difficult to provide direct instructional support as their children enter more advanced courses, and families who have not gone to college themselves may not feel equipped to provide other kinds of direct support, such as suggestions of specific schools to apply to or using online college application systems. In addition, families often find that schools and community programs don't provide opportunities to be involved in more direct ways, especially at the school building. This is particularly true during middle school and secondary school. But throughout the school years, many families experience schools as unwelcoming, closed off, and hostile.

These experiences of schools are particularly pronounced for ethnic minority and low-income families, who are often seen as "others" by staff in an educational system that is based on a paradigm of white, middle-class values. Ethnic minority and low-income families often experience discrimination from, disrespect among, and culture clashes with school staff and as a result do not necessarily trust schools.[8] In part for these reasons, and in part due to cultural values about appropriate roles for parents and teachers, many ethnic minority families tend to be more involved in education at home than at school, through strategies such as conveying values and expectations, facilitating study time and habits, and monitoring both their children's and the schools' behaviors. This can cause painful misunderstandings between families and schools, especially because many families are already doing valuable things to support their children's self-regulation for college that go unnoticed by practitioners. (It is important to point out that patterns of involvement vary across racial and ethnic groups; space constraints prevent a detailed discussion here of the edu-

cation values and school experiences of specific racial and ethnic groups beyond illustrative examples.)

Providing a Foundation for College-Going Identity and Motivation

Even less visible to practitioners than the ways in which they
support self-regulation, families also influence their children's
postsecondary pathways through their influences on identity
and motivation. For example, when families show that they believe their children are capable of high achievement, their children are more likely to set high goals, work hard, and persist in
the face of academic challenges. Not surprisingly, these behaviors translate into higher achievement. While we don't know of
any studies that have specifically followed this chain of events
to college enrollment and success, this is a logical next step. As
another example, when families place a strong value on learning and effort, their children are more likely to set the kinds
of mastery-oriented goals that we described in chapter 5. And
families can also send messages about the intrinsic value of
higher education not only directly through conversations but
by the actions they take. This is illustrated in a report produced
by the Bridgespan Group, which found that parent-student
college visits increased the odds that a young person would enroll in college.[9]

In chapter 5 we described how important it is that youths'
goals for college-going be about more than just making family
members proud. However, families' goals and expectations can
instill a value for higher education in their children, help youth
begin to envision a college-going future, and get them on a
path to taking ownership of their own goals and responsibilities. This is a powerful mechanism for helping young people
get and stay on the path to college and may be particularly

central for young children whose self-images and future plans are just beginning to develop. The role of family expectations and pride is illustrated by a young person named Aileen, who is quoted in Kathleen Cushman's book series *First in the Family*, which shares the stories of first-generation college students:

> My identity in my house, 'cause I come from a big family, is "the one that goes to college, the one that's trying to do something for her life." My brother's the one with the three kids who live with us, my other sister's the single mother raising two kids on her own, my other sister's only nineteen with a one-year-old son, and the other one is working in food services, the same job like my mother. Everybody looks at me, they're proud of me. Just to know that somebody is proud of you makes you even reach for more.[10]

In our experience, these kinds of encouragement and expectations are common among successful first-generation college students. And they are often driven by cultural values. For example, many immigrant families have made significant sacrifices and taken risks in order to help their children get a good education. Studies have shown that many youth whose parents have immigrated from Asian and Latin American countries both view it as an important part of their identity and feel a strong responsibility to take advantage of these opportunities and live up to their parents' expectations. And as several historians and researchers have pointed out, African American culture historically places a very high value on education as a route to success.[11]

However, families' cultural values for education are sometimes not seen by educators, such as the fact that Latino cultures often stress a broader view of education that includes moral and interpersonal as well as academic development. Worse, practitioners misinterpret families' values and behaviors as indicating a lack of support for education when, in fact, many families and the cultures to which they belong place a very high value on education. For example, researchers Nancy Hill and Kathryn Torres, who have reviewed the literature on Latino families' educational involvement, point out that Latino families' "use of manual labor to teach the importance of school may be misinterpreted as a devaluation of school," and that the trend of Mexican parents keeping their children out of school beyond the traditional December school vacation in order to celebrate holidays with family in Mexico has spurred the threat of legal action.[12]

Practitioners operating on a white, middle-class paradigm may also not be knowledgeable about the ways in which cultural identities shape how families *share* their educational values. For example, it is common for families from Latino cultures to share their values through *consejos* (cultural narratives in the form of advice, cautionary tales, verbal encouragement, and stories), including *dichos*, or traditional proverbs. Some researchers have referred to the role of *consejos* and *dichos* as "social resources" or "moral capital" because they build young people's values and motivation.[13] Susan Auerbach, who conducted an ethnographic study of Latino families participating in a school-based college access program in Los Angeles, found that families' moral support, including their consejos, were the primary way that parents shaped youths' college goals, postsecondary planning, and other developmental processes that we have described in previous chapters. Parents relied on this form of support in part because they saw it as a more appropriate and important way of supporting postsecondary success than instrumental support, but also because they often did not have the cultural capital, such as knowledge of the U.S. educational system, to provide more instrumental support.

Because teachers, counselors, and other practitioners receive little to no training in working with families, they are often not adequately prepared to understand these cultural differences and to work in ways that acknowledge and build on families' strengths and supports. For the same reasons, practitioners are often unprepared to deal with the cultural conflicts that arise for young people and their families around going to college, such as the clash between families' cultural values for interdependence among family members and an ethos in American higher education that emphasizes moving away from home and acting independently. Conflicts between academic and family responsibilities, such as caring for younger siblings and helping support the family financially, pose challenges for many high school and college students, but can be especially difficult for students from cultures that value family interdependence, such as many Latino and Asian cultures. This is demonstrated nicely in a teaching case prepared by Lad Dell for the Harvard Family Research Project that tells the story of a young woman named Marisela.[14]

Marisela is a high-achieving high school student with dreams of attending medical school. She emigrated to California from El Salvador with her three younger siblings and her mother, Claudia, who left her home country and her husband to "escape the war and give her children a better life." After excelling in challenging coursework and volunteering at a local hospital, all while caring for her siblings to help her hard-working and appreciative mother,

who holds down two jobs, Marisela is accepted at several competitive universities on the East Coast, including Johns Hopkins, which has offered her a strong financial aid package and flown her out for a campus visit.

While excited about the possibilities, Marisela is conflicted about going so far away from home, because she knows that her family relies on her. She wonders if she should attend UC Riverside, which doesn't feel like the right fit for her but is about ninety minutes from her family. Her mother, who is "torn between her hopes for her daughter and her dependence on her," wonders if "maybe it's better that she go to the nearby community college." She says, "I'm so proud of Marisela . . . I want her to be successful and have it easier in life than I did, but I don't know if going away to school will be good for her. She's so young and I worry about her safety and how she'll be treated . . . maybe it's better that she [stay close to home]."

❖　❖　❖

These kinds of family-school conflicts can also pose challenges after students have entered college. Researcher Vivian Tseng has studied such conflicts in an ethnically and socioeconomically diverse group of college students. While many students face competing responsibilities from families and academics, Tseng hypothesized that such conflicts would be especially pronounced for students from immigrant and ethnic minority families, who often have more family obligations and responsibilities based on cultural, logistical, and emotional factors that range from helping parents navigate a new culture and its systems to students' desires to repay parents for the sacrifices they have made to come to the United States. Tseng's study found that students with strong "family obligation attitudes" (for example, a strong desire to reflect well on the family) had higher achievement in college.[15] In contrast, students with high "family behavioral demands" (such as providing financial support through part-time jobs or logistical support through translation services) had lower achievement in college. These findings illustrate the complexity of culturally driven values and behaviors in the face of the dominant American education paradigm: some types of family obligations can be beneficial, whereas others can pose conflicts that make it difficult for students to achieve to their potential and to their families' high aspirations.[16]

Being aware of and respectful toward these kinds of cultural conflicts is essential for practitioners to work effectively with both families and their adolescent children in helping them access and succeed in higher education. While it would be impossible for anyone to possess intimate knowledge of every young person's culture, never mind differences among families within a culture, it is both possible and desirable for practitioners to work with families in a mindful and culturally sensitive way. As we will describe in more detail, this requires that they become reflective about their own cultural values and social positions, sensitive to the negative experiences of many families, and committed to listening to, honoring, and working with the cultural values of families. Even when families' values and goals are not in sync with schools or organizations, the goal is not to change families, but rather to work with them in ways that are respectful of differences and that recognize and build on their assets.

OPPORTUNITIES FOR PRACTICE

Valuing families' contributions to the college-going process, and building relationships with families in order to support and enhance their contributions, is an essential strategy for supporting college access and success. But in our work and that of our colleagues, we have seen that partnering with families is often one of the most complex and challenging parts of the process, one that is often marked by misunderstanding and sometimes conflict. In some cases, these misunderstandings even lead some practitioners to believe that parents just don't care. However, we know that this is rarely the case. Lots of research backs us up, showing that the vast majority of parents have high hopes for their children and want to support them to succeed in school and in their adult lives.

There is no one-size-fits-all approach to working with families, because all families have different strengths and needs and because college can mean and require different things for different families. Teachers, counselors, and afterschool providers who excel in working with families recognize and respect families' diversity, not just in terms of cultural and socioeconomic backgrounds, but in terms of their unique hopes, dreams, and values for their children and, especially, the unique assets and strengths that they bring to supporting their children's college-going goals. They aim to counteract many families' experiences of discrimination on the basis of race, class, and language; fears (sometimes well-founded) that their children will be labeled or tracked if they reach out for help; and the fact that American schools are based on and reinforce white, middle-class cultural values and assumptions that do not necessarily match those of all families. They are also thoughtful about the very real barriers that hamper family-school relationships, including logistical challenges such as schedule conflicts and lack of transportation, language barriers and a lack of translation services, and competing demands especially in the face of financial stress and low-wage work.

The only way to truly overcome these barriers is to adopt a framework of mutual responsibility for family-practitioner relationships and to create a culture that truly welcomes and engages with families. This means that practitioners, as well as families, have to reach out, take an active role, and commit to ongoing efforts to build relationships. Many schools and programs miss this step and rely on an insufficient "if you build it, they will come" approach. Have you ever stood in an empty room on a family college night and wondered, "Where are the parents?" Think back. Did you have a foundation of trust and respect with families in your school community? Did you understand their needs and their potential barriers? Recently, we have seen encouraging signs that more programs are thoughtfully addressing some of the logistical barriers by providing dinner and childcare during evening events, sharing college-going information in local supermarkets on the weekends rather than expecting families to come to school-based events, and using text messages rather than emails because this form of communication is more common and comfortable for families in their schools. But these kinds of strategies need to become the norm, and they need to be accompanied by a true commitment to the hard work of ongoing communication and relationship building in order to truly pay off. Creating a family-friendly school, program, or initiative requires a combination of supportive policies, practices, and beliefs among leaders, practitioners, and support staff, such as administrative assistants, who often have more contact with families than anyone else on the staff.

A complete discussion of building a welcoming environment for families is beyond the scope of this chapter.[17] Nonetheless, a few important strategies can get the ball rolling and lay the foundation for more in-depth work:

- *Don't be color blind or culture blind.* To form and maintain positive relationships with families from diverse racial, ethnic, and socioeconomic backgrounds, practitioners need to be aware of their own cultural location and social status and how they differ from families'. This includes understanding power differentials between professionals and families and making efforts to reduce them by listening to families' concerns, providing translation services and other logistical supports that make it possible for families to be involved, and using simple strategies such as making sure that they don't sit behind desks when talking with parents. In addition to understanding their own cultural values and assumptions, practitioners should intentionally look for and aim to understand families by asking questions, avoiding assumptions, and focusing on strengths and assets. Seeing difference is important and beneficial; seeing deficits is not. This strategy is important for direct service practitioners and also for the program and school administrators responsible for professional development and staff evaluations, who can embed these approaches.
- *Commit to ongoing, accessible communication.* Communication is an essential part of building relationships with families in general, and for promoting their involvement in college-going specifically, especially because many families of first-generation college-bound students lack information about how American higher education works and

what students need to do to succeed. Communication between practitioners and families is not necessarily easy or free of conflict, but it is essential in order to promote trust, build relationships, and share information in both directions. Communication should be frequent, respectful, and offered in multiple ways (in person, in writing, texting, social media) and from multiple people (school staff, community members, neighbors). Information should be available not just at college night events and on Internet Web sites but at school resource centers, in community-based locations such as churches and social service agencies, and even at businesses that employ large numbers of youths' parents. Ensuring that communication is accessible to parents of all reading abilities and languages is essential. Translation should be provided for all written and oral communications so that all families can be full participants. While translation services can be expensive and difficult to procure, they are worth the investment and can sometimes be obtained through creative strategies such as giving students academic credit in order to provide them or asking bilingual families who already have strong relationships with the school to provide them as a volunteer service to the school and their communities.

- *Invite families to be involved in college planning events.* Including family members in college awareness opportunities such as college visits and other exploratory activities can engage them in a crucial part of the process and simultaneously reinforce youths' beliefs about parental support for college-going. Involving families in this way sounds like a simple strategy—and it can be—but it is often overlooked. Research shows that outreach from schools is one of the strongest predictors of whether and how families get involved, especially ethnic minority families. For many of the reasons we have cited, many families do not trust schools, and it may take many invitations to convince them to participate. In addition, it may require reducing some of the logistical barriers that many families face, including the need for child care for younger siblings and flexible scheduling to accommodate the nonstandard hours of low-wage jobs. Inviting families that have already been involved to help plan future events and recruit other parents is also a useful strategy. And inviting families means more than simply asking them to show up; it also means genuinely welcoming them, asking for their input, honoring their contributions, and listening to their concerns.

- *Meet families where they are.* Practitioners who rely on families to come to them are usually disappointed. Families have a wide number of (often very good) reasons for not coming to schools or community-based events and meetings. Practitioners should seek opportunities to connect with families in the places that are most accessible and comfortable for families. These can include popular community gathering places, such as grocery stores, hair salons, and community centers, where practitioners can reach families either face-to-face or through distributing flyers and other information that families can pick up at their convenience. Community institutions such as churches and resource centers can be valuable partners in these efforts, either by providing venues for school staff to reach families or by conducting their own college information events. Practitioners can also consider conducting home visits, which have proven to be an effective strategy in building trust and strong relationships.

- *Create opportunities for families to connect with one another, either in groups or one-on-one.* Just as young people trust and learn from their peers, so do parents. Particularly for parents who come from cultures or neighborhoods not represented by most school staff, other parents may offer a unique sense of trust and rapport. Some college access programs incorporate the role of families' cultural identities by building relationships among families either through building parent social networks or facilitating one-on-one conversations. Often, such efforts involve parents whose children have gone to college sharing their experiences and perspectives with parents of high school students. The value of this approach is captured in *The College Track*, a video series that portrays several college access programs, including a GEAR UP program in South Texas that used a train-the-trainer model with parents. In this program, a parent coordinator trains parents to meet with other parents in the community and discuss their children's future education.[18] These parent outreach workers talk with other parents, help them think about saving for college, and talk with them about their children's college-going experiences. Programs like this can be beneficial but are not available or possible in all communities. In these cases, practitioners can ask parents of alumni or upper-class students to lead workshops or speak at college-focused events.
- *Facilitate family-youth discussions about college.* Many parents who have not gone to college themselves have high aspirations for their children and encourage them to go

to college, but do not know how to help them beyond talking about the importance of college. Practitioners can help by providing a list of questions for parents to ask their children about their future hopes, goals, and plans and about the steps they are taking to get there (such as what kinds of courses they are taking and if they are reaching out to counselors, college access programs, and others for help). Practitioners can also engage youth in these kinds of conversation by conducting projects in which youth interview their parents or other adult family members about the family's hopes and goals for the young person's future. By adding elements like video and writing, this project can also build self-regulatory and creative skills.

- *Create opportunities for youth and families to work together.* Families are more likely to participate in and benefit from educational events, including college access events, when their children are actively involved, but the active youth role often gets lost. Practitioners can work with families and young people simultaneously by organizing student-led conferences. Student-led conferences appeal to families, address young people's needs for responsibility and agency, provide opportunities to build leadership and self-regulation skills, and help to form a team philosophy in which all parties are on the same page. Practitioners can also engage families in college visits. If possible, they can take family members along on campus visits. If this is not possible, they can involve families by helping youth share what they learned through a photography exhibit, making and editing a video, or writing a journal or letter.

CONCLUSION

Essential Principles for Incorporating Adolescent Development

Throughout this book, we have called for a paradigm shift. In our view, a new approach to college access and success that intentionally incorporates adolescents' social, emotional, and cognitive development holds great promise for reaching youth who might not otherwise pursue or achieve a college degree. The need for this shift is clearer today than ever before in order to redress serious inequities in higher education, which lead to persistent and pernicious economic and social inequality. We know that many professionals are already working tirelessly to support young people. In the face of large caseloads, competing demands, and increased but still insufficient resources, adding this layer to the work may seem like a tall order. But in our experience, applying a developmental perspective can actually make working with young people easier because it illuminates some of the reasons that these youth engage in behaviors that we adults find mystifying, and doing so can keep us from heading down paths that result in dead ends.

Changing the paradigm is as much about changing how we work as about changing what we do. Small changes in everyday practice can make a big difference. This is especially true when the many people who reach youth work together and when they are supported by the policies and resources that make this work possible, from legislative guidance to funding to training and capacity building.

Embarking on this new approach begins with considering some key principles that cut across the specific developmental processes we described in the preceding chapters. These principles are applicable to professionals working in a variety of roles and settings, and they also provide guidance for policy makers, funders, and other field leaders. While every effort makes a difference, youth are most likely to benefit from the developmental perspective when these principles are applied consistently in all of the settings, programs, and practices where they live and learn. For everyone, then, the following principles provide a place to start as well as an opportunity to reflect on progress:

- College-going skills translate into college-staying skills
- Developmental processes build on one another
- Activities that support college-going don't necessarily talk about college
- Youth must be agents of their own futures
- Youths' needs (not adults') must be central
- It takes a village to build a successful future
- Changing the paradigm requires practices, not just programs
- Applying developmental theories and research takes training and support

College-Going Skills Translate into College-Staying Skills

College-going, like adolescent development in general, is a continuous and ongoing process. Because support structures for youth tend to be focused at discrete points along the college pipeline, it is easy to lose sight of the fact that college aspirations, preparation, access, and success are interconnected. And the skills that support college access also support success during and after college. This is certainly true of academic skills, as indicated by research showing a strong correlation between high school GPA and college persistence. But it is also true for goals, self-regulation, and identity. Throughout the book, we have provided strategies that can be used by people in many different roles and settings, but we have also provided strategies for those who work at specific points in the college pipeline. Even for those who do not work at these specific points in the process, understanding these approaches can help them connect their work within a broader, longer-term strategic approach.

Developmental Processes Build on One Another

There is a growing consensus in psychology, neuroscience, medicine, and other fields that social, emotional, and cognitive skills influence one another and that they cannot be understood in isolation. Likewise, the specific developmental processes that we have described in this book are interconnected, and the competencies required for college-going build on one another. As Nobel Prize–winning economist James Heckman has put it when writing about early childhood education, "skill begets skill."[1] For this reason, it is important to approach development holistically rather than focusing college access efforts solely on one process, such as motivation. Of course, specific programs or efforts may choose to focus on one or two elements, but these efforts should be seen as part of a larger developmental approach.

Because the connections among developmental processes are circular rather than linear, it may make sense to start at different points in the cycle with different youth, depending on individuals' unique situations and needs. At the same time, certain processes may provide a strong foundation that makes the development of others smoother or easier. This is why we have structured the book as we have. We began with identity because we see it as foundational for all of the other developmental processes we described and, indeed, for all aspects of the college-going process (including academic and financial aspects). In our experience, identity is often left unexplored by practitioners. This may be because identity is such a complex issue. Alternatively, it may be due to concerns about violating young people's privacy or because of discomfort with starting conversations about race, ethnicity, and class. But such conversations are essential. Even college access efforts that focus on one or a few specific components of adolescent development must pay careful attention to how youth think about themselves and incorporate the meaning they make of experiences into their current and future self-images.

Activities That Support College-Going Don't Necessarily Talk About College

As we've pointed out, many existing programs tend to serve those youth who already envision college-going futures for themselves but need additional support to achieve their goals. What about the other youth who could succeed in college but don't picture themselves as college-goers, don't have the initiative or self-regulatory skills to seek out services, or don't have the social capital to reach out to mentors? To improve educational equity, programs and practices need to reach young people earlier. This means not only reaching them at younger ages but reaching them at earlier stages in the development of identity, motivation, and self-regulation. Even before talking with young people about whether they plan to attend college, adults should help them to develop self-efficacy, set and pursue intrinsic goals, persist in the face of challenges, and develop the self-regulatory skills that will help them succeed at anything they choose to do. Through supporting these processes, which are not specifically about college-going, adults can set the stage for more young people to benefit from the dedicated college access efforts that focus on aspirational, academic, and other supports. Supporting these broader developmental processes requires engaging and collaborating with a broad range of stakeholders and settings, particularly those whose work is not dedicated to college access per se.

Extracurricular activities, service learning opportunities, and internships have much to offer; they provide opportunities for youth to develop interests and master skills. Through these activities, youth come to make meaning about themselves, about the nature of the world, and about possibilities for the future. They need to have opportunities to explore a wide range of interests and talents, because neither they nor adults know what will inspire them. In fact, research from the afterschool field suggests that the adolescents who have the best academic, social, and health outcomes are those who participate not in one all-encompassing program but in a quilt of programs and activities. At the same time, youth need to have opportunities to focus and to develop their skills in a few key areas, because experiences of competence and mastery are essential for developing and maintaining intrinsic motivation, mastery goals, engagement, and the ability to make commitments over time. In their book *Understanding Youth*, Michael Nakkula and Eric Toshalis describe this as supporting possibility development with skill building, and they point out that neither is possible without the other.[2]

Youth Must Be Agents of Their Own Futures

At all stages in the process, young people need to be active agents of their own development and of college-going in order to leverage and benefit from the supports available to them. For example, developing effective goals is clearly an essential part of motivation for college, but youth also need to be able to turn those goals into action by assuming ownership and responsibility for them. When young people have agency, they feel that they have control over their own destinies, and they are more likely to take positive, constructive actions to help them accomplish their goals.

Developing agency is particularly relevant and important during adolescence. Obviously, young children need more structure because they are not capable of assuming responsibility for their own goals and behaviors. This is why parents have to pack their backpacks for them and why educators need to intervene in social situations that involve exclusion or teasing. But as they progress through early and late adolescence, young people become more and more capable of assuming responsibility and directing their own behavior. This does not mean that adults play no role in adolescents' agentic beliefs and behaviors. Adults' scaffolding is essential. Adolescents develop agency through opportunities and relationships in their daily lives that allow them to make choices, assume increasing levels of responsibility, and develop skills. Adults cannot give young people agency, but they can and should provide opportunities for young people to develop it. As we have heard Courtland Lee, counselor educator and professor, point out, youth development and counseling efforts cannot "empower youth," as they often claim, but they can set up conditions, experiences, and contexts in which youth become empowered.

Promoting agency requires that adults seek and utilize opportunities for young people to take responsibility and take action. This includes being aware of how adults' own actions can get in the way, especially when they want to make things easier for youth or help ensure that they don't drop the ball at key points in the college-going process. Promoting agency also requires that those working in schools, youth programs, student employment settings, and other settings provide interactive opportunities that make youth an active part of the process of learning and skill building. Too often, adolescents are in settings where material is presented to them didactically and they are expected to master it in passive ways. Research on motivation as well as other fields, such as cooperative learning, show that the more interactive the experience, the more likely young people are to enjoy it, learn it, and internalize it. This is just as true for college access practices as it is for academic instruction. And while adults may think that the experiences they offer youth are interactive and designed to build agency, there is often room for improvement. For example, many programs aim to promote youths' motivation for college by providing opportunities for them to visit college campuses and observe classes or visit dormitories. But in our opinion, youth would develop more motivation and agency from opportunities to actually engage in the day-to-day activities of a college student. This is why experiences like dual enrollment courses, in which high school students take college courses for high school credit, can be very powerful.

Youths' Needs (Not Adults') Must Be Central

Promoting agency and ownership requires that adults be vigilant about putting youths' needs ahead of their own. While this point is often taken for granted, we believe that it needs to be made explicit, and that a failure to make it so can undermine many of the strategies we have presented. Many, if not most, educators and youth workers enter their fields out of a desire to help others. While certainly laudable, we have seen this desire to help unintentionally and often subconsciously give rise to a need to feel needed that can distract practitioners from the real goal of young people's success. The most common manifestation that we see of this is the well-meaning adult doing too much *for* youth rather than working *with* them or helping them to be challenged. Another is adults trying to impose their own goals and wishes for a young person rather than helping him create and discover his own path. In our experience, this sometime leads youth to act out of a desire to please counselors, teachers, or other adults. As we discussed in chapter 5, going to college for someone else's sake can backfire in the long run.

To temper these well-intentioned but counterproductive tendencies, we practitioners need to realize that the college-going process is not about us. Using reflective techniques and practices is essential for ensuring that we aren't letting our own needs, biases, and assumptions interfere with young people's development. As teachers ourselves, we often ask graduate students to reflect on their own lived experiences and on how those experiences might shape their work with youth. This begins with examining why they have entered this work and what they bring to it, and it emphasizes becoming attuned to their own racial, ethnic, and cultural identities and worldviews and how these may be different from those of the youth with whom they work. We believe that this kind of reflection is a career-long, and indeed a lifelong, process.

One reason that reflective practice is so valuable is that it allows practitioners to model for young people self-awareness, which is a key part of identity development. Youth form their own identities based in part on messages they receive from those around them. Through reflective practice, practitioners' conversations with youth are less likely to take the form of "This is what I did" and are more likely to be framed as "This is who I am, and, as a result, I did these things." The latter reinforces the importance of understanding oneself and shows that different people can take different pathways to arrive at some of the same goals and outcomes.

In addition to engaging in reflective practice, practitioners can and should be explicit with young people about their respective roles in the college-going process. There is a missed opportunity when a college-bound young person says, "I couldn't have done this without you," and adults around him don't challenge that statement. Here is an opportunity to say, "Yes, you could have," and a chance to help him identify the steps he took that allowed him to set and reach his own goals.

It Takes a Village to Build a Successful Future

When counselors, teachers, youth workers, community members, families, and peers work in collaboration to provide consistent messages about and support for college-going, young people are more likely to have a clear direction, more likely to access all of the supports they need, and less likely to fall through the cracks. This requires that many people and organizations act as partners in college access and success. American policies and programs for younger children espouse a "whole village" approach and aim for a web of supports, including services for parents, early child care and education programs, community activities, and others.

Our hope in writing this book is that practitioners will not only make changes in their own interactions with youth but will also adjust to how they work with other adults. In some cases, this shift may come from identifying the resources and supports that already exist and connecting the dots among them so that youth and their families can more easily access them and benefit from them. In other cases, the shift may come from working with other practitioners and leaders to build support systems and networks to promote college access.

At the individual level, practitioners can help young people find and leverage multiple supportive people who can facilitate their college-going paths. One of the reasons this is so valuable is because it is hard to predict just who is going to be the best match for which student at any given time. For one young person, it might be a teacher who has a unique window into her strengths and interests that, when developed, serve as a foundation from which to build a college-going path. Another youth might find support from a coach or afterschool leader, because she might have a close relationship with that adult or feel less concerned about being evaluated and judged than she would with her teachers. Yet another may find his strongest connections within his community—from his neighbor who owns the bodega on the corner, for example. These relationships influence college-going identities by introducing youth to people with whom they can identify and see future possibilities, familiarizing them with educational pathways they never knew possible, and connecting them to programs and services that form their self-concept. To leverage all of these opportunities, college access efforts should not aim to identify one or two partners who are best positioned to or most effective in providing support, but rather to see this work as helping young people create a network of supports.

Who those other people are, however, can vary quite a bit. Teachers play an especially significant role in supporting young people's motivation and self-regulation. Robert Pianta, who has studied classroom quality, has found that teachers can— and should—be a vital source of motivation for students; in fact, his research on classroom quality has found that teachers' levels of "motivational support" constitute one of the most important determinants of student success. Pianta has found that teachers influence motivation through a combination of practices, including showing students that they care about them, providing opportunities for choice and challenge, and making schoolwork relevant to their lives and futures. In addition, family outreach coordinators, school social workers, and staff from external programs and community agencies are all valuable sources of support, and they may be better positioned to reach some youth and families than traditional college access staff. For example, family outreach coordinators have existing relationships with families, and helping them engage families in college planning in a way that is aligned with other efforts can create both more efficiency and consistency. Family-focused staff can also work with families to identify the kinds of social and logistical supports that families need in order to best support their children's current and postsecondary success, from family health services to English and job skills classes for parents. In many cases, these resources exist but youth, their families, and their school staff do not know how to access them.

In addition to helping individual youth leverage support, leaders and policy makers can also "build the village" by creating or connecting with community-level initiatives. Building support systems can range in scope and scale, from building college-going cultures school- or organization-wide to creating community-wide initiatives. Whether at the individual or community level, efforts to help young people leverage support could benefit from engaging a few sectors and professional roles that have not traditionally been involved in college access but that are becoming more invested in this work.

As most practitioners can attest, partnership and coalition building is not without its challenges. In addition to the commonly acknowledged logistical challenges, territoriality and role boundaries frequently pose challenges. This can occur for many reasons. As we noted earlier, practitioners sometimes become so focused on helping or feeling useful that they lose sight of the importance of encouraging help and support from others. Some practitioners don't trust some of the "others" in young people's lives, or they simply aren't aware of what they have to offer. In addition, many nonprofits feel pressure from funders and policy makers to demonstrate their impact, leading them to take sole ownership of the process or to focus on protecting their limited resources. Whatever the cause for these barriers and boundaries, adults need to move beyond them and focus on what youth really need: a constellation of supports.

Changing the Paradigm Requires Practices, Not Just Programs

While community-wide initiatives and college access programs play unquestionably important roles, supporting the developmental processes that influence college-going must be part of adults' daily interactions with young people. The identity, motivational, and other processes we've described in this book develop over time and operate in all of the settings and moments of youths' lives. Because they do not develop within the confines of programs' hours or walls, adults must support and leverage them in ongoing ways and as part of all of their interactions, not just those focused on college.

Many of the recommendations and strategies we've described can be easily implemented in everyday practice. For example, teachers can support motivation by becoming attentive to praising effort over ability; so too can counselors and community mentors when talking with students about their schooling and employment experiences. Similarly, practitioners should continually work to build trust with their students and mentees and be on the lookout for opportunities that allow youth to explore their interests, self-reflect, and think about who they are and what they value. Maximizing these opportunities requires being developmentally aware, but it doesn't necessarily require more resources.

One of the advantages to applying a developmental perspective to daily practice is that the benefits can extend to multiple domains, including students' academic and personal development. As we noted above, academic, social, and personal development are highly interdependent. Failing to see these connections results in missed opportunities to support all of the processes involved in college-going, including the academic, aspirational, and financial aspects that are the domain of more traditional college access efforts. By employing a developmental perspective in a continuous way, from classrooms to hallway interactions to programs, adults can build young people's capacities to develop multiple skills that they need for college.

Applying Developmental Theories and Research Takes Training and Support

It is commonly said that leaders are made, not born. The same could be said about successful youth practitioners. Helping young people attain a college degree, especially those young people who face the most barriers to higher education, takes training. While this is true of many aspects of the work, it is clearly true for applying theories and research about adolescent development. Just because we have all been adolescents ourselves, or because many of us have worked with adolescents for years, it doesn't mean that we know the details of how and why adolescents act, think, and feel the way they do. Even those who have some training in adolescent development may not necessarily know how to make connections between this information and college-going.

Unfortunately, developmental theories and research are rarely considered in either pre- or in-service training programs for counselors, teachers, administrators, and youth workers. And, when it is included, it is seldom presented with connections to college preparation and planning. One of the consequences of this is that many practitioners rely on their own personal experiences with college-going or those of previous students in advising young people. We have seen many well-intentioned practitioners end up applying a one-size-fits-all approach rather than differentiating their supports and services to individuals' unique needs, goals, and pathways. As we described in chapter 3, when young people hear the stories of how others have shaped successful college-going paths, this can help them envision a college-going future for themselves; this can be particularly powerful when the adolescent and the college graduate share racial, ethnic, and other elements of identity. However, when young people hear about only one pathway, they may not be able to place themselves in that pathway and may even foreclose on the possibility of college. And, as we described in chapter 6, it may be more difficult for them to envision the multiple pathways and strategies for overcoming obstacles that can help them plan successfully for college and persist when some routes become blocked.

This is one of the reasons that we strongly encourage undergraduate and graduate training programs to incorporate more coursework in adolescent development, along with practicum experiences that help young people link adolescent development principles with their experiences in schools and communities. For example, counselor education programs (which do include some training in adolescent development) might consider strategies to link their existing developmental training with college counseling. This might include introducing stand-alone college counseling courses that specifically integrate adolescent development. Conversely, it might include discussing college-going in existing adolescent development courses. Training programs for professionals in other roles (e.g., teachers, social workers) will likely differ in emphasis and structure but can and should also find ways to teach and incorporate principles of adolescent development. As we have demonstrated in this book, teachers can incorporate many principles of adolescent development into their daily work in ways that promote student achievement, along with college-going goals and behaviors. For example, the authors of *The Road Less Traveled* report from the National Council for the Accreditation of Teacher Education call for teacher training programs to integrate principles of development in courses across the curriculum (as opposed to addressing development only in one dedicated course) and to create opportunities for preservice teachers to apply and discuss developmental principles and research into their field-based experiences, such as student teaching placements.[3]

While preservice programs are ideal places to introduce practitioners to developmental theories and their applications to college-going behaviors, in-service training is also essential, both because preservice programs are limited in the amount of time and experiences they can offer and because incorporating developmental knowledge, like development itself, is an ongoing process. National organizations that provide professional development, including those focused on college, such as the College Board, National Association for College Admissions Counselors, and National College Access Network, and those focused on youth development, such as the National Afterschool Association and the Cooperative Extension Service, might consider expanding training topics to include adolescent development. As the lines between school and nonschool supports become blurred due to extended school day initiatives, community schools, and other nontraditional approaches to education, it is also worth thinking about shared opportunities for professional development that cut across organizational boundaries and professional roles. In-service training and conferences that bring together professionals from different backgrounds allow all participants to learn from one another and to broaden their perspectives beyond what is traditional in their specific disciplines. They also provide an opportunity for practitioners to make and implement plans for working collaboratively (partnering to create programs, sharing recruitment strategies, helping youth access multiple kinds of programs and resources).

Shifts in preservice and in-service training programs would be strengthened by policies that support these changes. For example, accrediting bodies should adopt specific requirements that ensure school counselors and other educators gain knowledge of developmental processes that influence college-going behaviors. Likewise, most licensing boards regulate professional development requirements for licensure renewal. Changes to these requirements that reflect attention to adolescent development or links between postsecondary planning and developmental processes will go a long way toward helping schools meet statewide goals. With these types of training well established, states and districts can integrate developmental principles into the evaluation of school staff. Beyond policies that govern licensing, policy makers might consider block grants and other funding opportunities that can give schools and other organizations the flexibility to support professional development in creative ways across professional roles (school counselors, teachers, youth workers). This kind of interdisciplinary approach provides multiple benefits, including the opportunity for participants to see how multiple domains of development are connected, to learn from others who have a different perspective, and to learn how to leverage efforts from other fields. Such approaches can also increase efficiency in the face of limited resources.

A WINDOW OF OPPORTUNITY

The strategies we have described in this book are all small pieces in the large puzzle of educational equity. Incorporating an understanding of adolescents' social, emotional, and cognitive development is not about any one single process, strategy, or program. It is about approaching college access and success from a different and more holistic perspective.

The time is ripe for this change in perspective, because the conditions are right, the knowledge base is defined, and the need is clearer than ever before. The political and structural supports available today have created a window of opportunity for helping more young people get to college, thrive once there, and achieve the individual and societal benefits that higher education has to offer. At similar moments in history, our country has made significant strides toward equity in higher education. Now that we have another window of opportunity, what will our contribution be? Our hope is that it will be not one policy or program but a new approach that meets all young people where they are in order to help them get to where they want to be.

NOTES

Introduction

1. William C. Symonds, Robert B. Schwartz, and Ronald Ferguson, *Pathways to Prosperity: Meeting the Challenge of Preparing Young Americans for the 21st Century* (Cambridge, MA: Pathways to Prosperity Project, Harvard Graduate School of Education, 2011).

Chapter I

1. National Center for Education Statistics (NCES), "The Condition of Education 2011," NCES document no. 2011-033 (Washington, DC: Government Printing Office, 2011).
2. *Charting a Necessary Path: The Baseline Report of the Access to Success Initiative* (Washington, DC: Education Trust and National Association of System Heads, 2009).
3. David T. Conley, *College Knowledge: What It Really Takes for Students to Succeed and What We Can Do to Get Them Ready* (San Francisco: Jossey-Bass, 2005).
4. Sarah Hooker and Betsy Brand, *Success at Every Step: How 23 Programs Support Youth on the Path to College and Beyond* (Washington, DC: American Youth Policy Forum, 2009), 5.
5. Watson S. Swail and Laura W. Perna, "Pre-College Outreach Programs: A National Perspective," in *Increasing Access to College: Extending Possibilities for all Students*, ed. William G. Tierney and Linda S. Hagedorn (Albany: State University of New York Press, 2002), 15–34.

6. "Graduate Course Information," National Association for College Admission Counseling, www.nacacnet.org/CareerDevelopment/Resources/Pages/Graduate.aspx.

7. Jane A. Leibbrand and Bernadine H. Watson, *The Road Less Traveled: How the Developmental Sciences Can Prepare Educators to Improve Student Achievement—Policy Recommendations* (Washington, DC: National Council for Accreditation of Teacher Education, 2010).

8. Anthony Carnevale, Nicole Smith, and Jeff Stroh, *Help Wanted: Projections of Jobs and Education Requirements Through 2018* (Washington, DC: Georgetown University Center on Education and the Workforce, 2010).

Chapter 2

1. BYAEP collaborators: ZUMIX, Hyde Square Task Force, Medicine Wheel Productions, The Theater Offensive, and Raw Art Works.

2. Jeffrey J. Arnett, *Adolescence and Emerging Adulthood: A Cultural Approach*, 4th ed. (Upper Saddle River, NJ: Pearson Prentice Hall, 2010), 482, 10.

3. Robert Epstein, *The Case Against Adolescence: Rediscovering the Adult in Every Teen* (Sanger, CA: Quill Driver Books/Word Dancer Press, 2007).

4. Reed W. Larson, "Toward a Psychology of Positive Youth Development," *American Psychologist* 55, no. 1 (2000): 170–183.

5. Karen Pittman, Merita Irby, Joel Tolman, Nicole Yohalem, and Thaddeus Ferber, *Preventing Problems, Promoting Development, Encouraging Engagement: Competing Priorities or Inseparable Goals?* (Washington DC: Forum for Youth Investment, Impact Strategies, 2003).

6. Richard M. Lerner, Jackie V. Lerner, and Erin Phelps, *Waves of the Future: The First Five Years of the 4-H Study of Positive Youth Development* (Medford, MA: Institute for Applied Research in Youth Development, Tufts University, 2009).

7. Caroline Hoxby and Christopher Avery, "The Missing 'One-Offs': The Hidden Supply of High Merit Students for Highly Selective Colleges" (paper, American Economic Association, San Francisco, January 3, 2009).

8. Larson, "Toward a Psychology," 170.

9. *America after 3 PM.* (Washington, DC: Afterschool Alliance, 2009).

10. Larson, "Toward a Psychology," 170.

Chapter 3

1. The full eight stages of Erikson's theory include: trust versus mistrust; autonomy versus shame/doubt; initiative versus guilt; industry versus inferiority; identity versus role confusion; intimacy versus isolation; generativity versus stagnation; and ego integrity versus despair. For a detailed description of these stages and its application to educators, see Michael J. Nakkula and Eric Toshalis, *Understanding Youth: Adolescent Development for Educators* (Cambridge, MA: Harvard Education Press, 2006).
2. Henri Tajfel, *Social Identity and Intergroup Relations* (Cambridge: Cambridge University Press, 1982), 528.
3. Roberto G. Gonzales, *Young Lives on Hold: The College Dreams of Undocumented Students* (New York: College Board, 2009).
4. Howard B. London, "Breaking Away: A Study of First-Generation College Students and their Families," *American Journal of Education* 97, no. 2 (1989): 144–170.
5. Joel M. Hektner, "When Moving Up Implies Moving Out: Rural Adolescent Conflict in the Transition to Adulthood," *Journal of Research in Rural Education* 11, no. 1 (1995): 3–14.
6. Jeannie Oakes, *Critical Conditions for Equity and Diversity in College Access: Informing Policy and Monitoring Results* (Los Angeles: University of California All Campus Consortium on Research for Diversity, 2003), 5.
7. Melinda Merchur Karp, *Learning about the Role of College Student through Dual Enrollment Participation* (New York: Community College Research Center, 2007).

Chapter 4

1. Richard W. Auger, Anne E. Blackhurst, and Kay Herting Wahl, "The Development of Elementary-Aged Children's Career Aspirations and Expectations," *Professional School Counseling* 8, no. 4 (2005): 322–329.
2. *The College Track—America's Sorting Machine: Who's In and Who's Out,* DVD, prod. Alice Markowitz, Round Table, Inc. (Princeton, NJ: Films for the Humanities and Sciences, 2004).
3. Daphna Oyserman, Kathy Terry, and Deborah Bybee, "A Possible Selves Intervention to Enhance School Involvement," *Journal of Adolescence* 25, no. 3 (2002): 313–326.
4. Claude Steele, *Whistling Vivaldi and Other Clues to How Stereotypes Affect Us,* 1st ed. (New York: W. W. Norton, 2010).

Chapter 5

1. This term is inspired by the similar phrase "summer melt," which college admissions counselors use to describe the phenomenon in which students expected to matriculate in the fall choose another college or university over the summer.
2. Karen D. Arnold, Shezwae Fleming, Benjamin L. Castleman, Mario A. DeAnda, Katherine L. Wartman, and Philip Price, "The Summer Flood: The Gap Between College Admission and Matriculation Among Low Income Students" (paper, American Educational Research Association, New York, March 27, 2008), 12.
3. Ryan D. Hahn and Derek Price, *Promise Lost: College-Qualified Students Who Don't Enroll in College* (Washington, DC: Institute for Higher Education Policy, 2008).
4. Lisa S. Blackwell, Kali H. Trzesniewski, and Carol S. Dweck, "Implicit Theories of Intelligence Predict Achievement Across an Adolescent Transition: A Longitudinal Study and an Intervention," *Child Development* 78, no. 1 (2007): 246–263.

Chapter 6

1. Sara E. Stoutland, *How Students Are Making It: Perspectives on Getting Through College from Recent Graduates of the Boston Public Schools* (Boston: Boston Foundation, 2011), 29.
2. Ibid.
3. Angela L. Duckworth, "The Significance of Self-control," *Proceedings of the National Academy of Sciences* 108, no. 7 (2011): 2639–2640.
4. Steinunn Gestsdottir and Richard M. Lerner, "Positive Development in Adolescence: The Development and Role of Intentional Self-Regulation," *Human Development* 51, no. 3 (2008): 202–224.

Chapter 7

1. Nicholas A. Christakis and James H. Fowler, *Connected: The Surprising Power of Our Social Networks and How They Shape Our Lives* (New York: Little, Brown and Company, 2009).
2. Susan P. Choy, Laura J. Horn, Anne-Marie Nuñez, and Xianglei Chen, "Transition to College: What Helps At-Risk Students and Students Whose Parents Did Not Attend College," in *Understanding the College*

Choice of Disadvantaged Students, ed. Alberto F. Cabrera and Steve M. La Nasa (San Francisco: Jossey-Bass, 2000), 45–63.

3. Pamela Ellis, *Addressing the Shame of Higher Education: Programs That Support College Enrollment and Retention of African-American Males* (San Francisco: Level Playing Field Instititute, 2004).

4. Lillian Chiang, Carla D. Hunter, and Christine J. Yeh, "Coping Attitudes, Sources, and Practices among Black and Latino College Students," *Adolescence* 39, no. 156 (2004): 793.

5. Luther B. Otto, "Youth Perspectives on Parental Career Influence," *Journal of Career Development* 27, no. 2 (2000): 111.

6. Nancy E. Hill and Diana F. Tyson, "Parental Involvement in Middle School: A Meta-Analytic Assessment of the Strategies that Promote Achievement," *Developmental Psychology* 45, no. 3 (2009): 740–763.

7. Nancy E. Hill and Ruth K. Chao, *Families, Schools, and the Adolescent: Connecting Research, Policy, and Practice* (New York: Teachers College Press, 2009).

8. Nancy E. Hill, "Undermining Partnerships Between African-American Families and Schools: Legacies of Discrimination and Inequalities," in *African American Children and Mental Health,* ed. Nancy Hill, Tammy Mann, and Hiram E. Fitzgerald (Santa Barbara, CA: Praeger, 2011), 199–230; Nancy E. Hill and Kathryn Torres, "Negotiating the American Dream: The Paradox of Aspirations and Achievement among Latino Students and Engagement between their Families and Schools," *Journal of Social Issues* 66, no. 1 (2010): 95, 106.

9. William Bedsworth, Susan Colby, and Joe Doctor, *Reclaiming the American Dream* (N.p.: Bridgespan Group, 2006).

10. Kathleen Cushman, *First in the Family: Your High School Years* (Providence, RI: Next Generation Press, 2005), 5.

11. Hill, "Undermining Partnerships."

12. Hill and Torres, "Negotiating the American Dream," 106.

13. Mariella Espinoza-Herold, "Stepping Beyond Sí Se Puede: Dichos as a Cultural Resource in Mother/Daughter Interaction in a Latino Family," *Anthropology and Education Quarterly* 38, no. 3 (2007): 260–277; Susan Auerbach, "'If the Student Is Good, Let Him Fly': Moral Support for College among Latino Immigrant Parents," *Journal of Latinos and Education* 5, no. 4 (2006): 275–292.

14. Lad Dell, *Making a Decision about College: Should I Stay or Should I Go?* (Cambridge, MA: Harvard Family Research Project, 2003).

15. Vivian Tseng, "Family Interdependence and Academic Adjustment in College Youth from Immigrant and U.S.-Born Families," *Child Development* 75, no. 3 (2004): 966.

16. Interestingly, this study also found that students from immigrant families had higher academic motivation than their peers, but not higher grades. What explained the gap between motivation and achievement were differences in family demands: students from immigrant families spent, on average, fifteen more hours per week than their peers on family responsibilities.

17. For more detailed discussion of and strategies for family-school relationships, several resources are available, including Anne T. Henderson, Karen L. Mapp, Vivian R. Johnson, and Don Davies, *Beyond the Bake Sale: The Essential Guide to Family-School Partnerships* (New York: New Press, 2007); Jo Beth Allen, *Creating Welcoming Schools: A Practical Guide to Home-School Partnerships with Diverse Families* (New York: Teachers College Press, 2007); Heather B. Weiss, Holly M. Kreider, M. Elena Lopez, and Celina M. Chatman Nelson, eds., *Preparing Educators to Involve Families: From Theory to Practice.* (Thousand Oaks, CA: Sage, 2005).

18. *The College Track—America's Sorting Machine: Expect the Best,* DVD, prod. Alice Markowitz, Round Table, Inc. (Princeton, NJ: Films for the Humanities and Sciences, 2004).

Conclusion

1. James Heckman, "Schools, Skills, and Synapses," *Economic Inquiry* 6, no. 3 (2008): 289–324.

2. Michael J. Nakkula and Eric Toshalis, *Understanding Youth: Adolescent Development for Educators* (Cambridge, MA: Harvard Education Press, 2006).

3. Jane A. Leibbrand and Bernadine H. Watson, *The Road Less Traveled: How the Developmental Sciences Can Prepare Educators to Improve Student Achievement—Policy Recommendations* (Washington, DC: National Council for Accreditation of Teacher Education, 2010).

ACKNOWLEDGMENTS

Just like getting to college, writing a book takes a constellation of supports. We are grateful for all of the people and resources that have helped to make this book possible and have allowed us to shine a spotlight on the deeply important issue of helping more first-generation college-bound youth find and succeed on a college path. First and foremost, we thank the many young people, families, and colleagues who have inspired this book, including those whose stories are adapted for use in the case studies.

We greatly appreciate the colleagues who contributed to this book in various ways and stages of development, from conception to review to moral support. In particular, we thank Nancy Hill, Stephanie Jones, Robin Jacob, Ann Coles, Tom Hehir, Priscilla Little, Holly Kreider, Sara di Bonaventura, Ana Martinez-Aleman, and Gretchen Brion-Meisels. Along with other colleagues at the Harvard Graduate School of Education, we thank Dean Kathleen McCartney for her support for this project. This book would not have been possible without the support of Karen Bottari, Kristina Harrison, and Deborah Teo; we thank them for their time and willingness to contribute. To

Caroline Chauncey and her colleagues at the Harvard Education Press, we are grateful for your wise counsel and encouragement.

Both of us feel indebted to our families for their ongoing support and cheer. Mandy is especially grateful for her husband, Toby, whose encouragement and support have enabled her to develop and grow in ways she couldn't have imagined, and for her daughters' endless love and laughter. Suzanne is, as always, deeply thankful for her husband Chris's patience and unceasing emotional and instrumental support and for her parents' quiet but constant help and pride.

ABOUT THE AUTHORS

Mandy Savitz-Romer is a faculty member and director of the Prevention Science and Practice program at the Harvard Graduate School of Education. Her professional experience has allowed her to link research to practice in the field of school counseling, specifically as it relates to college and career readiness for first-generation college students. She has held previous positions at the Boston Higher Education Partnership, Boston University, Boston College, Simmons College, and the Boston Public Schools. As a former urban high school counselor, Savitz-Romer is particularly interested in how schools and districts structure counseling support systems and college planning efforts to reach all students. Her research interests include college access and success for first-generation college students; school counselor training and development; youth development; and preK–16 partnerships and policy. She holds a master's degree in school counseling from Boston University and a PhD in higher education from Boston College.

Suzanne M. Bouffard is a researcher and project manager at the Harvard Graduate School of Education, where she focuses on applying research on child and youth development to practice and policy. Her work has focused on social and contextual factors that support learning and educational success, including out-of-school time and youth development programs, social and emotional learning programs, and family-school-community partnerships. In her current role and her previous position at the Harvard Family Research Project, she has developed a specialty in communicating about these topics for practitioners through written publications and in-person professional development. She has taught at Boston University and Emerson College and has worked directly with children and youth from elementary school through college. She earned a PhD in developmental psychology from Duke University, where she was a J. B. Duke Fellow and a University Scholar and won an Outstanding Dissertation Award from the American Educational Research Association.

INDEX